THE
tinkering
workshop

T0304451

THE
tinkering
workshop

EXPLORE, INVENT & BUILD
WITH EVERYDAY MATERIALS

Ryan Jenkins

100 Hands-On **STEAM** Projects

Storey Publishing

The mission of Storey Publishing is to serve our customers by
publishing practical information that encourages
personal independence in harmony with the environment.

EDITED BY Deanna F. Cook
ART DIRECTION AND BOOK DESIGN BY Ian O'Neill
TEXT PRODUCTION BY Jennifer Jepson Smith

COVER PHOTOGRAPHY BY © Hesh Hipp, front (left, all but b.)
and back; Mars Vilaubi © Storey Publishing, front (all but t.l.,
2nd from t.l., 2nd from b.l.)
INTERIOR PHOTOGRAPHY BY © HeshPhoto, Inc., 1, 2, 8, 9,
11–13, 20 c. & t.r., 21 t. & b.r., 22 b. all, 23–27, 28 t.r. & m.,
30–31, 34, 35, 37, 43 t., 46 b., 47 castle, 49, 53, 56–57, 63,
66, 67, 71 b.r., 72, 73, 75–76, 78 b.l., 79 b.r., 80–82, 86, 89, 91
b.r., 92, 93, 96–97, 99 m., 101, 103, 107, 109, 111 all but m.r.,
112, 116–117, 120, 121, 122 b., 126, 127 all but b., 129, 132, 133,
134 l., 136–137, 140, 141, 153, 155, 159, 160 l., 162; Mars Vilaubi
© Storey Publishing, 3 (background) here and throughout, 5,
6, 7, 14, 15 all but hardware, battery & string, 17, 21 b.l., 22 t.
all, 28 b., 29, 32, 33 m. & b., 36, 38 all but b., 39 all but b., 40,
42 l., 43 b., 44 b., 45 r. & b., 47 background, 48 m., 50 t., 51
t., 59 b.l. & b.r., 60–62, 64, 65, 68 t.r., 74 l., 78 t., 85 l. & 85 r.,
88, 90, 91 all but b.r., 94, 98, 99 t. & l., 104, 106, 108 b., 110 t.,
113, 118, 119 t., 122 l., 125 b.l. & b.r., 127 b., 130, 131 t., m., r.,
134 r., 135, 138, 139 t.r., 144, 145 b., 146, 147, 148 m., 150 t.,
157, 161 r.
ADDITIONAL PHOTOGRAPHY BY © A secret club, 18 t.l. & b.l.;
© Aaron Kramer, 151 t.r.; Airam Dato-on/Unsplash, 148 b.; Amy
Snyder © Amy Snyder, 131 b.l.; Amy Snyder © Exploratorium,
142 l.; Annie Spratt/Unsplash, 124 t.; © AOME1812/
Shutterstock.com, 15 hardware; © The Book Worm/Alamy
Stock Photo, 150 b.; Carl Milner in association with Playful
Anywhere CIC, 85 b.; © Casper1774 Studio/Shutterstock.com,
39 b.; CHUTTERSNAP/Unsplash, 133 moon; Dan Cristian
Păduret/Unsplash, 45 m.l.; © donatas1205/Shutterstock.
com, 38 b.; © elisa galceran garcia/Shutterstock.com, 151 b.;
Emma Louise Comerford/Unsplash, 70; © Exploratorium by
Ryoko Matsumoto, 83 b.r.; © Exploratorium, 54 b., 55 b., 78
b.r., 79 t.r. & b.l., 83 t.l., 95, 105 b., 114, 149 b., 151 t.l., 154 b.;
Gianandrea Villa/Unsplash, 142 b.; © Gumpanat/Shutterstock.
com, 124 b.; © Hoopla Haven/Shutterstock.com, 111 m.r.;
Institute for Applied Tinkering/Creative Commons Attribution
4.0 International, 48 b. & t.; Ivory/Public domain/Wikimedia
Commons, 84 b.; Jay Kettle-Williams/Unsplash, 142 t.r.; Jie
Qi, 134 b.r.; Jode Roberts, 99 b.r.; © JpegPhotographer/
Shutterstock.com, 110 b.; Courtesy of Liam Nilsen, 55 t.;
Courtesy of Live Oak School, 18 b.r., 19 t.; © MikeMartin/
Shutterstock.com, 59 m.; Nicole Catrett, 18 c., 19 all but t.;
© Oksana_Schmidt/Shutterstock.com, 125 m.; © piksik/
Shutterstock.com, 20 b.; © PS stock/Shutterstock.com, 156
t.; © Raihana Asral/Shutterstock.com, 15 string; © Remigiusz
Gora/Shutterstock.com, 15 battery; Robert Ruggiero/
Unsplash, 58; Ryoko Matsumoto, 102 m.; Courtesy of Sam
Haynor, 42 r.; Courtesy of Shih Chieh Huang, 143; Simon
Kadula/Unsplash, 44 screws; © Song II/Shutterstock.com,
145 t.l.; © SRT101/Shutterstock.com, 149 t.; © Teerapon
metta/Shutterstock.com, 69; Teslariu Mihai/Unsplash, 125
t.r.; © TuktaBaby/Shutterstock.com, 139 b.r.; © Vladimir
Mulder/Shutterstock.com, 50 b.; © Wonderful Idea Co., 33 t.,
46 t., 51 m. & b., 54 t., 68 c., 71 b.l., 74 r., 83 t.r., 84 t., 102 t. &
b., 105 l. & r., 107 inset, 108 m., 115, 119 b. & m., 122 t.r., 123 t.,
139 c., 145 t.r., 154 t., 156 b., 160 r., 161 l.; VoltPaperScissors
.com, 123 b.; Yaakov Winiarz/Unsplash, 148 t.

Text © 2024 by Ryan Jenkins

Safety Note:
When using hot or sharp tools and materials, be sure to prepare
yourself, set up a clear workspace, and pay attention to what you
are doing. Take care to follow the safety tips in the first chapter
and on each project page as you play and explore.

All rights reserved. Hachette Book Group supports the right
to free expression and the value of copyright. The purpose of
copyright is to encourage writers and artists to produce the
creative works that enrich our culture. The scanning, uploading,
and distribution of this book without permission is a theft of the
author's intellectual property. If you would like permission to use
material from the book (other than for review purposes), please
contact permissions@hbgusa.com. Thank you for your support
of the author's rights.

The information in this book is true and complete to the best
of our knowledge. All recommendations are made without guar-
antee on the part of the author or Storey Publishing. The author
and publisher disclaim any liability in connection with the use of
this information.

The publisher is not responsible for websites (or their con-
tent) that are not owned by the publisher.

Storey books may be purchased in bulk for business, educa-
tional, or promotional use. Special editions or book excerpts can
also be created to specification. For details, please contact your
local bookseller or the Hachette Book Group Special Markets
Department at special.markets@hbgusa.com.

Storey Publishing
210 MASS MoCA Way
North Adams, MA 01247
storey.com

Storey Publishing is an imprint of Workman Publishing, a division
of Hachette Book Group, Inc., 1290 Avenue of the Americas, New
York, NY 10104. The Storey Publishing name and logo are regis-
tered trademarks of Hachette Book Group, Inc.

Distributed in Europe by Hachette Livre, 58 rue Jean Bleuzen,
92 178 Vanves Cedex, France
Distributed in the United Kingdom by Hachette Book Group, UK,
Carmelite House, 50 Victoria Embankment, London EC4Y 0DZ

ISBNs: 978-1-63586-809-8 (paperback); 978-1-63586-751-0
(paper over board); 978-1-63586-752-7 (fixed format EPUB);
978-1-63586-908-8 (fixed format PDF); 978-1-63586-909-5
(fixed format Kindle)

Printed in Guangdong, China through World Print on paper from
responsible sources
10 9 8 7 6 5 4 3 2 1

WP

Library of Congress Cataloging-in-Publication Data on file

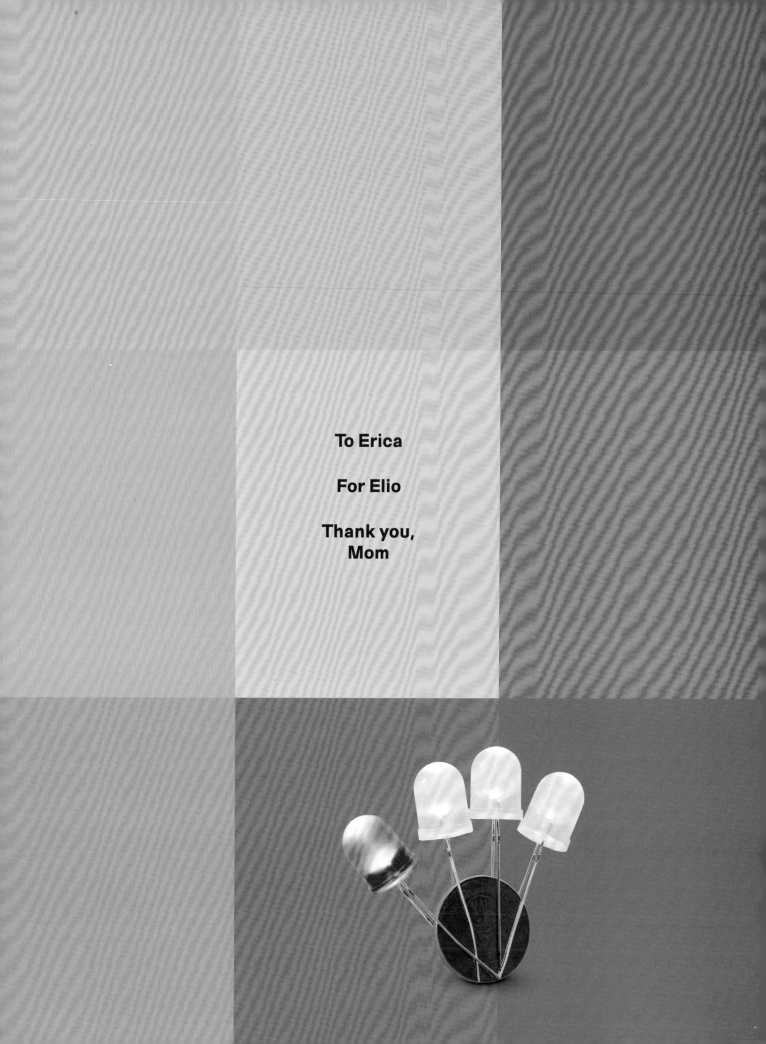

To Erica

For Elio

Thank you,
Mom

contents

welcome to tinkering!

Tinkering is a fun way to learn about the world around you. You get to play with materials, experiment, and work through ideas. This process is also called messing about, prototyping, improvisation, or making things up as you go along.

Tinkering can sometimes look like acting silly, making a mess, or giving a high five. It can also look like quiet thoughts, a furrowed brow, and a deep "hmmmm" as you try to figure out the next steps.

Tinkering can sometimes be hard work. Taking any idea from inside your head and putting it out into the world takes time, energy, and effort. As you flip through these pages, pull together your materials, and start building things, it might seem challenging. You'll need to take charge of your own experience and make choices about what to do next.

Soon, you'll get that good feeling that comes from creating something yourself. In the end, it doesn't matter if your hanging mobile leans crooked or your spinning automaton only turns in one direction. You have made something you can be proud of!

The more you tinker, the easier it becomes. You get used to remixing and improving your projects. You do research and get excited about what to try next. You get inspired by other people's work. Before long, you might build or invent something no one has ever thought of before.

Whoa, that feels cool!

Tinkering can start to spill over into the rest of your life. You'll look at challenges with an open mind. You'll get comfortable working with a team and sharing ideas. You might fall in love with an idea or get obsessed with finding the answer to a question. You'll discover you don't know all the answers.

These are amazing outcomes that are good for you and great for the rest of the world. We need people who can figure things out for themselves and not just accept the way something has always been done. That's how we can solve the big challenges of the future.

And you'll have some fun along the way!

—Ryan Jenkins

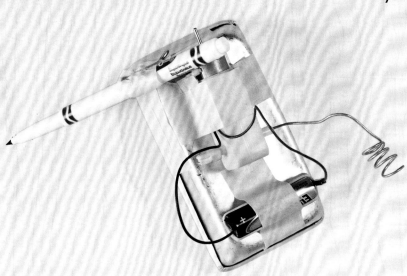

CHAPTER 1
get ready to tinker

As the maker, you get to create tinkering projects in your own special way—no one else's projects will look like yours! Just get to know your materials and start building.

start exploring

Get curious! How can you animate a cardboard animal or get a windmill to spin? There are many tinkering questions and many possible solutions! And who knows where you might end up? What you build will look different than the examples in this book. They may look more beautiful and work even better.

Let the materials launch your tinkering adventure. Whether you begin with a handful of screws, scrap wood, or plastic pipes, study your materials closely and let them inspire your tinkering projects. Get inspired by some of the ideas on each What You Can Do Right Now page.

Follow the Get Started steps for each of the 21 projects, then keep tinkering with Play & Explore and Going Deeper suggestions. While this book provides starting points, it's up to you to make (and break) the rules. You can decide when to keep working on your own and when to call for help.

Check out the STEAM Connections. Each tinkering exploration involves science, technology, engineering, art, and math. When you combine all of these elements, the results are often surprising—and amazing!

Keep a tinkering notebook. You never know when a good idea or a tricky question will arise. Keep a notebook handy for your tinkering explorations.

Connect your investigations to your passions. The possibilities are endless.

Mix it up. If you find yourself drawn to a range of tinkering explorations, try combining them to see what happens. An electrical windmill on the top of a fort would be an interesting innovation. Mix and match to see where your curiosity takes you.

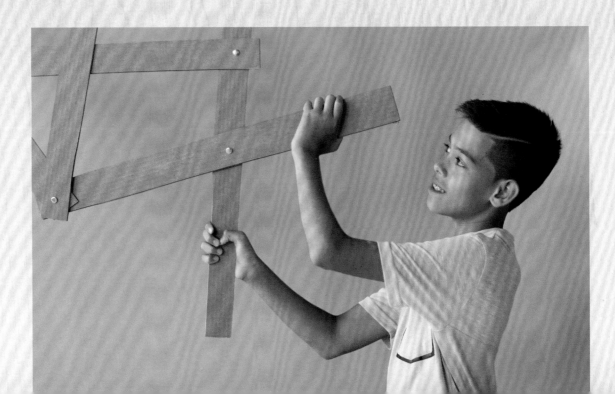

troubleshooting

As you work through your projects, you'll often find yourself facing problems: A tower starts leaning, a boat starts leaking, or your mind starts wandering. That's okay. In fact, it's a normal part of the tinkering process. Here are some problem-solving tips:

Break the problem into steps. Sometimes it helps to write down or draw everything. Make a list of what you've tried and what you want to try next.

Look closely at the parts. When something isn't working, take a close look at the materials. Maybe you need to add more glue, reinforce the structure, or make some other adjustment.

Find help. Ask a parent, friend, or sibling for help. Or look online for similar projects or for tips on using tools.

Work on something different. If you feel discouraged about one part of your project, change gears. For example, if you can't get a mechanism to work, focus on decorating it. When your hands are busy with something new, your brain often comes up with a solution to the problem.

Take a break. Reset with a short break, a walk outside, or a snack. Don't forget that you are in charge of your own tinkering process.

tinkering supplies

Look around for stuff you can use to explore, invent, and create. Each material opens new possibilities for tinkering. Throughout this book, you'll find ideas for what you can do right now with everything from screws to cardboard to garbage bags.

new materials

Your **local hardware store** is the place to get most of the materials and tools you'll need, such as masking tape, wood, screws, pipes, wire, bubble wrap, and more.

A **dollar store** is a great place to buy kitchen supplies, small hand tools, craft materials, paper, and containers for organizing your tinkering stuff. Search the aisles for other interesting materials that you can use in new ways.

At **craft stores**, you can find materials like googly eyes and pipe cleaners to give your project a sense of fun. You might also find reflective fabric and specialized tools.

If you have one nearby, browse a **restaurant supply store** for kitchen materials such as containers and utensils.

There are **specialty online shops** for things like motors, battery packs, alligator clips, LED lights, wiring, and other high-tech and low-tech electrical and electronic supplies.

recycled supplies

Look for tinkering supplies around your **house, garage, and recycling bin**. Finding new ways to reuse the things that you would otherwise throw away makes your projects more sustainable and unique.

Garage sales and swap meets are great places to find tools, wood, and hardware like screws and nails. Look for electronic toys, old typewriters, and rotary phones to take apart. Collect all the screws, wires, switches, and motors to use in your tinkering projects.

Look for **reuse stores or centers** to get surplus materials and supplies like corks, clothespins, marbles, and fabric. Search online for "creative reuse center near me" and see what comes up.

You can often find big **recycling bins outside furniture stores** with plenty of cardboard and packing foam you can take home. Start a cardboard collection area in your house or garage so you have supplies when you need them.

supply exploration

Use materials in unexpected ways.
A scrap of wood, a clothespin, or a plastic tube is made to be used for a specific purpose. But in the tinkering world, materials have life beyond their normal use. Try putting them to work in new ways.

Let your senses guide you. See, hear, feel, and even smell your materials. Knock a material with your knuckle to hear how it sounds, bend it to the point of almost breaking, and pick it up to feel its weight. All of these factors can help you figure out how you can best use this material in your work.

Notice patterns. Does cardboard bend a certain way under a heavy load? Do some tapes hold strong while others lose their grip? How much air can you put inside a plastic bag before it pops? How do different objects move in the wind? These are questions to answer as you tinker.

Find substitutions. If you can't find the exact part you were hoping for, look for similar materials and see if you can swap them out in your project.

make a tinkering station

Tinkering can happen anywhere— on a kitchen table, on the floor in your room, or even outside in a park. If you have space in your room, garage, or basement, you can set up a more permanent tinkering station. Here are some good starting points.

TABLE: Set up a table or other sturdy surface to tinker on. Be sure it doesn't shake or wobble and that it's big enough to fit your projects and materials.

BROWN CRAFT PAPER: Cover your tabletop with brown craft paper. The paper protects the table from glue, scratches, and paint. It also doubles as scrap paper you can use to sketch or take notes.

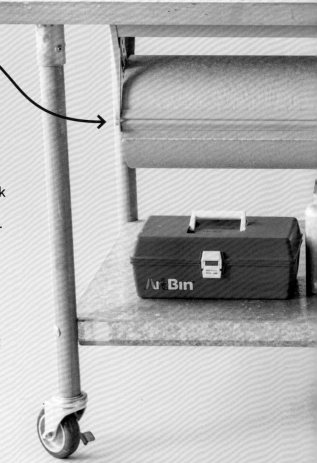

Tinkering Pop-Up

If you don't have space for a permanent tinkering spot, your workshop might be pop-up style, such as a cardboard box to hold supplies and a tray—something to set up before starting a project and clean up before dinnertime.

SHELVES: Stock tinkering supplies on shelves beside or below your tinkering table. Use bins or containers that are see-through, if possible, so you can easily grab the right material.

TOOL ORGANIZER: Keep an eye out for tool chests when you are at garage sales or thrift stores. A pegboard box like the one shown below is a great way to store tools. It can be opened up to display all your tools, too.

EXTRAS: Add whatever else you might want to keep you feeling energized and focused in your tinkering space. Perhaps a little green plant, a water bottle, a portable speaker, or your favorite snacks?

LIGHT: You'll need good light so you can see what you are doing. A desk lamp with a bright bulb works well.

POWER STRIP: A power strip on top of the workspace comes in handy so you don't have to crawl under the table to unplug your glue gun or reach your rechargeable batteries.

CHAIR: Set up a chair or stool to sit on as you work on your projects. It should be at a height that allows you to comfortably reach the table.

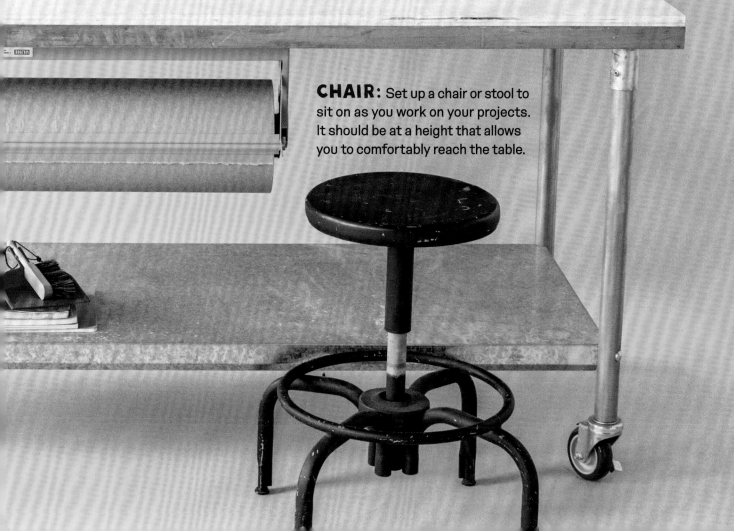

GOING DEEPER

creative makerspaces

The best way to design your own workspace is to get inspiration from other tinkerers. Here are ideas from tinkerers **Lianna Kali** of the ChangeMaker Lab, artist **Nicole Catrett**, and **Kenn Munk** and **Annabelle Nielsen** of A Secret Club. What ideas can you take from each of these makerspaces?

Sewing Stuff
A Secret Club has a cupboard for sewing-related materials and tools.

Workshop Magic
The ChangeMaker Lab has a sturdy worktable, seating that is easy to move, and a drop-down power cord hanging from the ceiling.

Bucket Stool
Some tinkerers make stools out of buckets! They build comfortable cushions on the lids and keep supplies inside.

Creative Containers
Nicole has a collection of containers, large and small, including baskets, tins, magnetic pincushions, and even a set of mixing bowls she borrows from the kitchen. When she's working on a project, she fills the containers with materials and sets them out on a tray, just like paints on a painter's palette.

Label Bins

Material bins at the ChangeMaker Lab are organized and labeled by type, and you can see what's inside. A step-stool helps kids reach the higher shelves. Past projects are displayed on the top shelf above the materials.

Storage Stuff

Nicole uses a squeezy honey bear for dispensing wood glue; a plastic jug with a hole poked in the top to keep her yarn from getting tangled; a piece of wood with holes drilled in it to store and keep organized markers, pencils, and drill bits; and a magnetic pincushion to hold anything that is small and metal.

Sawhorse Workbench

Nicole made this workbench for her daughter out of an old cutting board that's screwed to a wooden sawhorse.

Tinkerer's Treasure

Nicole calls this basket her "treasure chest" and keeps it filled with inspiring materials. These include aluminum cans, boxes, tubes, cardboard of all shapes and sizes, tinsel, bits of wood, and recycled materials to use for tinkering projects.

snip & cut

Many tinkering explorations require cutting cardboard, wire, plastic, or recycled materials. The main cutting tools you'll need are **scissors**, **utility knives**, and perhaps a **rotary blade**.

If you have to cut a complicated shape, trace it with a pencil first. Consider making **relief cuts**, which are little snips from the edge of the material to the line you are cutting.

Before you begin cutting, practice on a scrap piece of the material to see how it feels to cut straight lines or curves.

Scissors

Find a pair of scissors that fits your hand and is easy to use. (If you're left-handed, get a left-handed pair.)

Rotary Blade

A rotary blade looks and works like a pizza cutter, but you use it to cut fabric or paper. Be sure to put the safety cover back on when you're done using it.

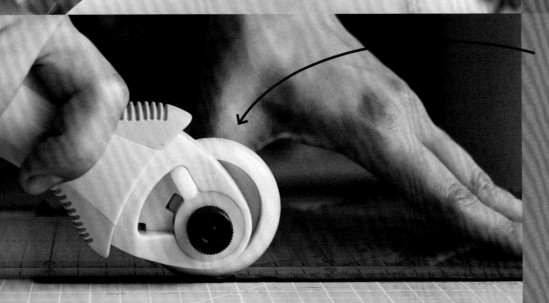

Utility Knife & Box Cutter

These blades are used for cutting cardboard and other flat, thin sheets of material. They are very sharp. The first time you need one, an adult should show you how to use it. Be sure to retract the blade when you're not using it.

When you use a utility knife, box cutter, or rotary blade, first put down a cutting mat or large piece of thin wood to protect your work surface. Hold the blade steady, and apply even pressure all the way through each cut.

Utility knives, box cutters, and rotary blades are sharp, so follow the safety instructions and work with an adult until you feel comfortable using them.

Hand Protection

Before making a cut, look at where your hand holding the material is placed. If your fingers are too close to the path of the blade, move them. If you want, wear cut-proof gloves, which add an extra layer of protection.

Eye Protection

When you use a utility knife, you should always wear safety goggles to protect your eyes from sharp scraps, like pieces of plastic or metal.

A sharp blade is safer than a dull blade. Be sure to replace any blade that looks dull or damaged.

Try an Awl!

An awl is a useful tool for punching holes in materials like cardboard, plastic, or even fabric. It has a pointy tip and a comfortable grip. When you make a hole, make sure you keep your hands away from the underside of the material where the pointy part pokes through.

attach the parts

Most tinkering projects will rely on two tools for attaching pieces together: **tape** and **hot glue**.

Masking Tape

Masking tape works for almost any purpose. It is easy to find, sticks well, and can be ripped into pieces of whatever size you need. It also comes in different widths and colors. Start with a roll of ¾-inch thickness.

More Types of Tape

You can try using clear packing or Scotch tape, removable gaffer's and painter's tape, or strong duct tape. Copper and aluminium tape conduct electricity. Electrical tape is useful for projects that have wires.

Tape Loops

Make a little loop of tape to stick on decorative elements. For things that need to be sturdy, make sure you have strong, overlapping pieces of tape.

To rip tape, pinch it with your index fingers and thumbs, then rotate one hand toward you and the other away from you.

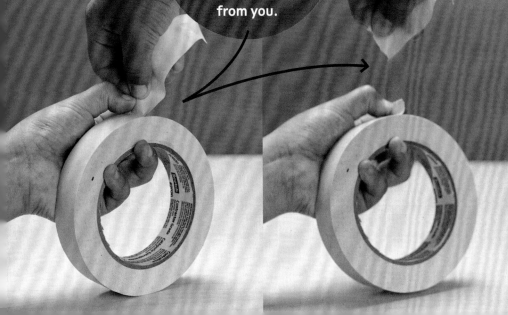

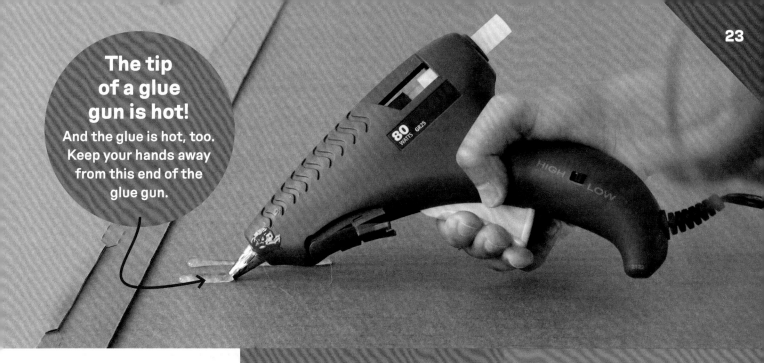

The tip of a glue gun is hot!
And the glue is hot, too. Keep your hands away from this end of the glue gun.

Tip: Start with a thin line of glue.

Hot Glue Gun

While you can use masking tape for most of the projects in this book, a hot glue gun will improve your tinkering experience. This simple machine has a hot nozzle and a stick of solid glue. A stream of hot glue comes out when you press the trigger. In less than a minute, the glue cools down enough to hold two pieces of material together.

Safety Tips

- The first few times you use a glue gun, make sure a responsible adult is around.

- Cover your work surface with paper or cardboard to catch drips.

- After you plug it in, let the gun fully warm up (depending on the model, this can take as long as 10 minutes). The gun is ready to use when the glue squeezes out easily.

- If you need to glue something small to something big, put the glue on the big piece first, and then stick the small piece onto it.

- Hot glue dries quickly but not immediately. Wait at least 10 seconds before handling any pieces you just hot-glued together.

- Don't forget to unplug the glue gun when you are finished. Don't leave the glue gun on the table when you are working. Put it in its holster on a separate table. It's very easy to accidentally get burned by placing your hand on a hot glue gun when you are reaching for supplies.

bend, cut & strip wire

Tinkering with metal wire to build structures or connect circuits? These tools and techniques will make it a lot simpler.

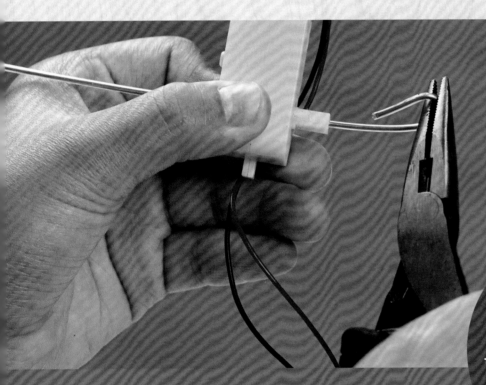

Cut Wire

Some round-nose pliers also can cut wire, like this pair. Put the wire into the neck of your pliers. Hold the other end of the wire in your hands and squeeze.

To make a loop, bend the wire into a gentle curve at one spot, then move your pliers a little further down the wire and bend it again. Repeat until the wire has bent all the way around in a circle.

Round-Nose Pliers

Round-nose pliers, also called jewelry or rosary pliers, are great for bending wire. Look for a good pair with a spring-loaded joint that easily opens and closes. Pick one that also can cut wire. Try a few at the hardware store to find the one that fits comfortably in your hand.

To bend wire, use the round-nose pliers to get a strong grip at the place where you want the wire to bend. Hold the rest of the wire in your other hand. Bend the wire by gently rotating your wrist, keeping a good grip on the wire with the pliers.

Wire Stripper

Use this tool to remove the plastic coating from the outside of a wire, revealing the metal part that makes electrical connections. Wire strippers come in different shapes and designs. Start with traditional wire strippers, which look like a pair of pliers with a row of holes of varying sizes in its mouth. Each hole is labeled with the gauge (size) of the wire it is able to strip.

Start Here

To use a wire stripper, match your wire to the appropriate hole in the stripper. Set the wire in the hole and squeeze the handles to hold it in place. Rotate the stripper to cut through the plastic all the way around the wire, then pull the wire out, leaving the plastic behind.

Wear safety goggles when cutting wire so that little bits of metal don't fly into your eyes.

drill & saw wood

Wood is a strong building material for tinkering projects. When you're working with wood, it's helpful to have both a power drill and a Japanese handsaw. Here's how to use both.

Safety Tip: Whenever you use a power drill or saw, wear goggles. Work on a table at a comfortable height so that you are not reaching up or down when you drill or saw.

Cordless Power Drill

Use this battery-powered tool with drill bits to make holes in wood and other materials. Or use it with driver bits to insert screws.

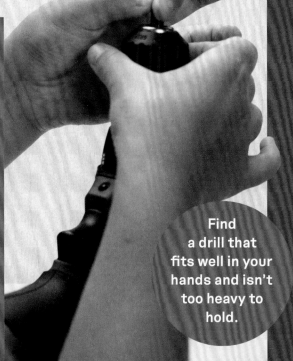

Find a drill that fits well in your hands and isn't too heavy to hold.

Japanese Handsaw

A Japanese-style handsaw works great for cutting wood. This type of saw cuts pieces of wood smoothly on the backstroke.

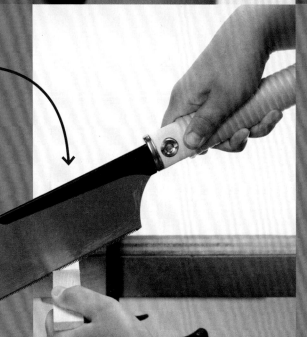

How to Drill a Hole

1. Clamp your wood to a table so it can't move around.

2. Choose a drill bit and secure it in the drill. Hold the drill over the wood, with the drill bit on the spot where you want the hole and your finger on the trigger. Place your other hand on top of the drill to hold it straight.

3. When you're ready, pull the trigger and press down gently to start making a hole in the wood. Work your way up to a faster drilling speed by squeezing the trigger more tightly.

How to Use a Handsaw

Clamp your piece of wood to the table. Mark the place where you want to cut with a pencil. Draw the saw blade over the penciled cut line a couple of times to start your cut. Then saw with smooth, even motions until you have cut the wood all the way through. Don't forget to save your scraps!

Use a Power Drill as a Screwdriver

1. Before driving a screw into wood, first drill a pilot hole—a hole that's slightly smaller than your screw. A pilot hole makes it easier to drive in the screw and keeps the wood from cracking.

2. Attach a flat-head or Phillips-head driver bit to your power drill to use it as a screwdriver.

3. Place the screwdriver bit on top of the screw and start the drill slowly.

Tip: Power drills have a button or switch to control the direction in which their bit turns. A clockwise spin will drive a drill bit or set a screw. A counterclockwise spin will remove a screw.

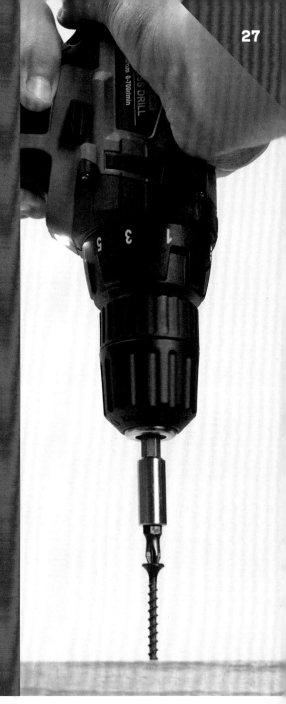

connect circuits

Some tinkering projects use electricity. Electricity always travels in a circuit, or loop. Once you know how to connect a circuit, you can use it to power small motors, light bulbs, and more. Here are a couple of tips and ideas for setting up electrical circuits. Work with an adult for these projects if it's your first time.

Safety Tip: Only tinker with projects that are powered by batteries. Wall power can be especially dangerous, so take extreme caution with any project that has to be plugged in.

Batteries

Battery power is measured in volts, and you should stick to less than 12 volts total for your circuits. Coin cell, AA, AAA, and 9-volt batteries are good options to start with. It's helpful to have your batteries secured in a **battery pack.** You can buy one or make your own battery holder with rubber bands, cardboard, and aluminum foil.

Safety tip: Coin cell batteries can be very dangerous if swallowed. Take care when working around younger siblings or pets.

Outputs

Any device that you activate with electricity is called the output of the circuit. Good outputs to experiment with are **motors,** lightbulbs, buzzers, and computer fans.

Wires

You'll need electrical wires for any circuit project. These wires are metal (a material that conducts electricity) and usually have a plastic coating.

Wire Connectors

Some electrical wires end in **alligator clips,** which can be easy to connect as part of your circuit. You can also connect wires with a soldering iron (see right), screw or snap terminals, aluminium foil, and metal or electrical tape.

Making a Circuit

Remember, electricity travels in a circuit, or loop. Your battery pack and output in your circuit should have two connectors: one to receive electricity, and one to send it back out. Attach wires from one device to the next to carry the electricity around the circuit.

Electricity travels best through metal, so every connection in a circuit should be metal-to-metal. Sometimes that means you'll need to strip the plastic coating from the wires to expose the metal inside (see page 25).

Once it's all connected, your motor or light will turn on. If it isn't working, swap the wires from the battery pack, change the batteries, or try a different output.

You can mount an output (like a light bulb) to a board and secure its wires to metal nails. Then it's easy to snap connectors onto the nails to complete the circuit.

Safety tip:
If you notice your circuit getting hot or you smell burning, disconnect the wires right away!

Soldering

Soldering is a technique for joining metals. You use a soldering iron to heat up a soft metal, called solder, until it melts. You apply the melted solder to the joint between metals, and as it cools, it solidifies, working like glue to secure the metals together.

Be sure to work with an adult the first time you use a soldering iron. Wear goggles, turn on a fan or fume extractor, and use lead-free solder. Hold the hot tip of the soldering iron between the two pieces you want to connect for about 10 seconds.

Solder comes in the form of a wire. Bring the tip of the solder wire to the tip of the iron. If it's hot enough, the solder should flow into the joint. Remove the solder wire and then the soldering iron.

CHAPTER 2
Constructions

What happens when you build bridges and structures with straws and clothespins, pile up wood scraps in zany towers, unfold a cardboard box hideout, or send a marble up, down, and around a chair?

CLOTHESPINS

Classic spring-powered clothespins, made with wood and wire, are perfect for many tinkering explorations. You can also experiment with clothespins made with plastic or metal. Look for clothespins at hardware stores, at supermarkets, or online.

A WORLD OF CLOTHESPINS

Can you find clothespins that are mini or giant? How about clothespins made of metal, plastic, or wood? See how many different sizes of clothespins you can find.

The largest clothespin in the world was sculpted by **Claes Oldenburg** in Philadelphia and is more than four stories tall!

What can you do with CLOTHESPINS right now?

A Third Hand

If you're gluing, soldering, or attaching pieces in some other way, you might need an extra gripper. Make a tool for that by attaching a clothespin to a piece of wire.

Clothespin Character

Use googly eyes, wire, or anything else you have around to make a character with a mouth that opens, teeth that bite, or ears that wiggle.

Quirky Racer

Add wheels to the ends of wooden skewers. Then make axles, experimenting to see which ones allow the skewers to turn freely inside the jaws of clothespins. Connect your wheel-and-axle assemblies to make racers. Test your quirky racers and watch how they roll.

Sign Holder

Glue a clothespin to a block of scrap wood so the grippy part is facing up. Place a tiny sign in the mouth of the clothespin.

Nail Holder

Save your fingers! Use a clothespin to hold a nail in place when you hammer.

build-it kit

You can get into the building mindset by creating a construction kit out of any two materials. Let's start with a kit made from clothespins and straws!

FIND THIS STUFF

Wooden clothespins | Paper or plastic straws

GET STARTED

1. Spread out a bunch of clothespins and straws on a table. Take a good look at all the ways they could connect to each other.

2. Start building with these two materials. Let your imagination take you in different directions.

PLAY & EXPLORE

Get creative and build one-of-a-kind sculptures out of straws and clothespins. Try building one with only right angles. Then try making a structure with no right angles. Anything goes!

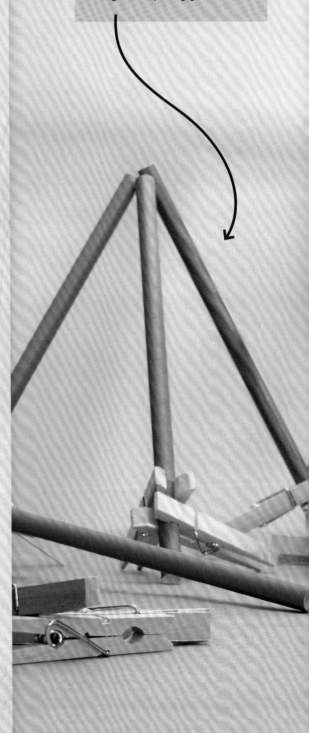

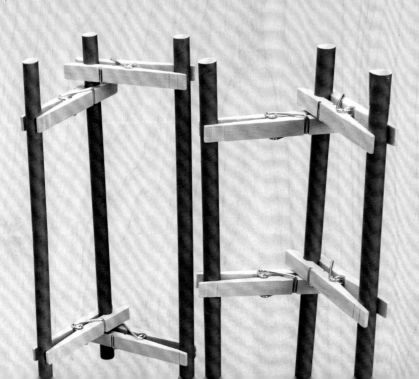

Think modularly. Consider your kit as a building system. Find a combination of two or three pieces that you like, make a lot of copies, and then see what you can build with those mini modules.

Tinkering is better together. Share your building kit with a friend and see what you can make when you combine your ideas.

Make small changes. What if you cut some straws in half? What new possibilities open up?

If you get stuck, take everything apart and start fresh.

Construct tall towers, stable bridges, and structures that look like they could be buildings of the future.

Do all the connectors work in the same way? Look for different ways to connect the pieces. For example, you can grip straws with the jaws of clothespins, but you can also thread a straw over the end of a clothespin.

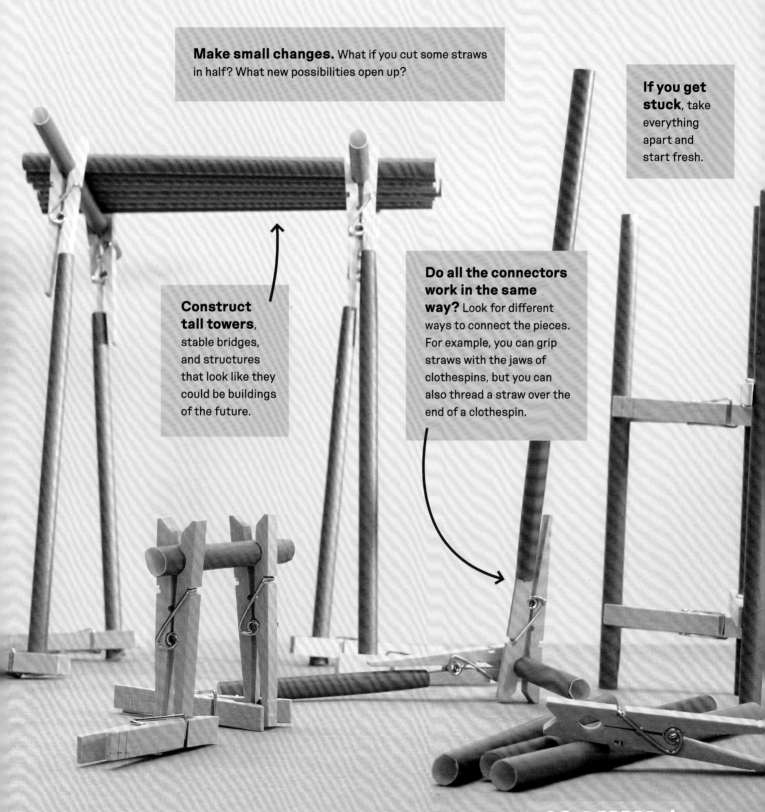

construction toy zone

Keep on tinkering with your own custom construction kits. Look around to find materials you can use to build what's in your imagination.

Build More Construction Sets

Pick two different materials to build with. How about building with clay and toothpicks?

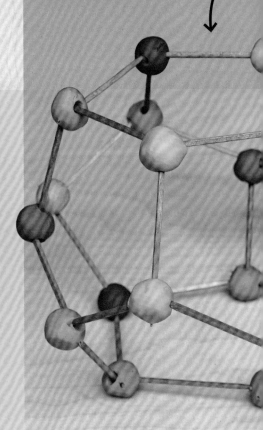

Toy Hack

Do you have any building toys? Take one of these kits and hack them with the addition of a second material. Clothespins and LEGO Technic beams are a fun place to start.

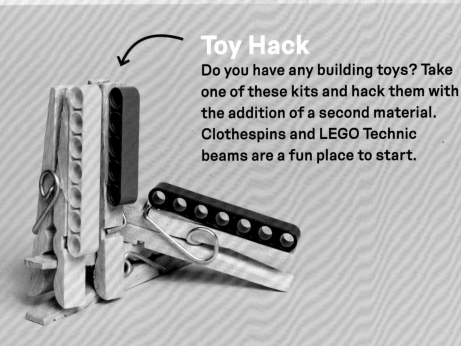

S·T·E·A·M Connections
STRESS & STRAIN

Any material, from clothespins to concrete, can support a certain amount of weight before it changes shape or collapses. The pressure on the material is called the stress, and the way the material cracks or bends is called the strain.

If a structure you build with your two-material construction kit sags or snaps under pressure, notice where it breaks down and swap out one of the materials to see how the change affects the strength of the structure.

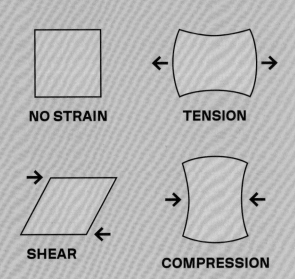

NO STRAIN

TENSION

SHEAR

COMPRESSION

Nature Set

Go outside and find some natural objects, like leaves and sticks, to build a clothespin construction kit.

WOOD SCRAPS

When you use scrap wood, you recycle material that would otherwise get thrown away, and you can make something unique and beautiful. Scrap wood is often irregularly shaped and can be used in many tinkering projects. Ask to use pieces from a furniture maker's woodshop scrap bin or the scrap bin in a hardware store or school.

IS IT HARDWOOD OR SOFTWOOD?

With scraps, you don't always know what kind of wood you're working with. Softwood comes from evergreen trees, like pine. Hardwood comes from trees that lose their leaves in the winter, like oak, walnut, or maple. Softwood is easier to cut, sand, and drill holes into. Projects built with hardwood last longer. It's not always easy to tell the difference, but you can look at the end (softwood should be less dense). Or try to scratch the wood with your fingernail (you can usually make a mark in softwood but not in hardwood). Smell the grain and see if you can tell different types of wood apart without looking.

What can you do with SCRAP WOOD right now?

Homemade Xylophone

Suspend short pieces of scrap wood between two longer pieces. Strike them with a stick or a xylophone mallet to make a scrappy musical instrument.

Domino Run

Create a chain reaction by lining up flat pieces in a long row. Tip the first block and watch the blocks fall one by one.

Drill, Screw & Nail Practice

Place a large piece of wood on the ground. Grab screws, nails, drill bits, a screwdriver, a drill, and a hammer. Fill the wood with screws and nails. Can you consistently drill, screw, and nail straight into the wood?

Sand It

Use sandpaper to restore wood that's roughed up, dirty, or painted. Start with sandpaper with a low number like 80 and work your way up to a higher number like 200. Sand with the grain of wood, moving in the same direction as the lines of dark and light. Try to sand with smooth motions across the block of wood and smooth the rough edges, too.

Scrappy Stacks

Stacking blocks provides hours of fun for tinkerers of all ages. As you engineer wood towers, you experiment with art, science, and balance.

FIND THIS STUFF

Scraps of wood in many different sizes | Cinder block, bucket, or stool

GET STARTED

1. Put a scrap of wood on the ground or on a table. Add another piece on top of that one.

2. Keep stacking and see how high you can go. It may seem simple, but it gets more challenging with each block.

3. Set a cinder block, bucket, or stool in your building space. Stack on this surface, too. How does your stack change?

Can you tell when the stack is about to fall? Is there anything you can do to rebalance the parts?

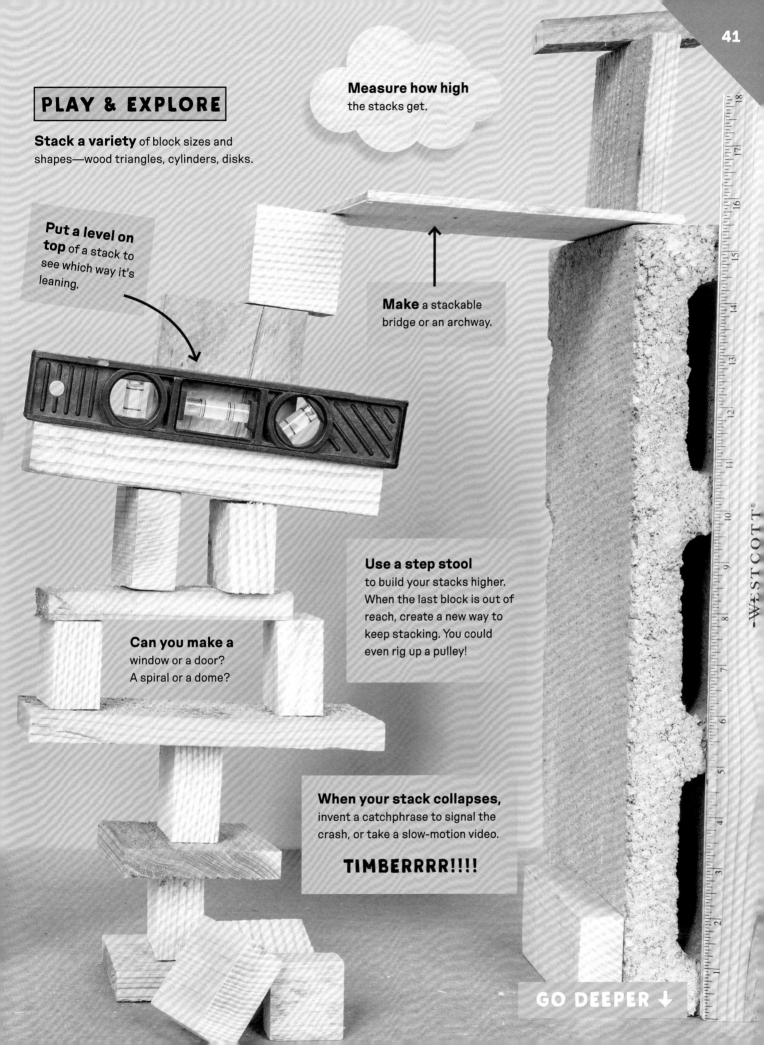

PLAY & EXPLORE

Stack a variety of block sizes and shapes—wood triangles, cylinders, disks.

Measure how high the stacks get.

Put a level on top of a stack to see which way it's leaning.

Make a stackable bridge or an archway.

Use a step stool to build your stacks higher. When the last block is out of reach, create a new way to keep stacking. You could even rig up a pulley!

Can you make a window or a door? A spiral or a dome?

When your stack collapses, invent a catchphrase to signal the crash, or take a slow-motion video.

TIMBERRRR!!!!

WESTCOTT®

GO DEEPER ↓

keep on stacking!

Change the variables to make stacks of all shapes, sizes, and colors.

Wood Stack Character

Draw or paint eyes, noses, and mouths on your blocks.

City Buildings

Stack blocks to make a city scene with little houses, skyscrapers, windows, doors, cars, and trees.

S·T·E·A·M Connections
CENTER OF GRAVITY

Creating stacks of stones, blocks, or everyday materials may seem simple, but as you build towers, you are investigating the center of gravity, the place where gravity acts on the object. Each time you add a block, you change the stack's size and shape, which creates a new center of gravity.

As you stack, try to sense where the center of gravity is with your hands, and guess where to put the block on the tower so that it doesn't fall.

Shadow Sculpture

Build a wood stack outside on a sunny day so it casts a shadow. Can you build a stack whose shadow looks very different from the stacked blocks? Can you build a stack to create a specific shadow picture?

Wobbly Stacks

Try a slightly harder version of tinkering with stackable objects by building an unbalanced table. Place a platform on top of a wooden or plastic half sphere. Then start stacking, and try to keep your structure stable.

SCREWS

Screws are used to hold two or more materials—wood, metal, plastic, even cardboard—together. They can be so tiny they need to be picked up with tweezers or so huge they are hard to lift. A screw is inserted into materials with a screwdriver that matches the size and shape of the screw head. You can also use a power screwdriver or a power drill with a driver bit (page 27). Buy screws at the hardware store, or take apart old structures or devices to find them.

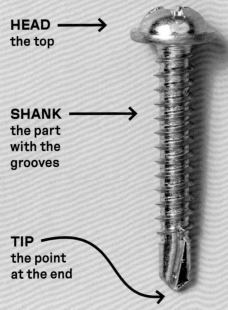

HEAD ⟶
the top

SHANK ⟶
the part
with the
grooves

TIP
the point
at the end

KNOW YOUR SCREWS

There are lots of different types of screws. Pay attention to the length, the size of the shank, and the type of head and tip. Different projects use different types of screws. The fort project on page 46 uses machine screws, which have flat tips. Combined with nuts and washers, they create a strong connection.

What can you do with SCREWS right now?

Study Screws

Grab a magnifying glass or a microscope and look at the head, shank, and tip of the screw. Can you figure out what material you are supposed to drive the screw into?

Test a Magnet's Strength

Find a magnet and see how many screws you can pick up with it.

Rain Stick

Make your own musical instrument from a large cardboard poster tube. Cover one end, then drive in screws of different sizes along all the sides, so the shanks are in the middle of the tube. Fill the tube part-way with dry rice or lentils, and cover the other end. Turn the rain stick over and over and listen to the sound.

Remove Rust

Test the best ways to remove rust from an old screw. Try out a small piece of aluminum foil dipped in lemon juice, cola, vinegar, or baking soda. Rub it on the rusty metal and see what works the best to clean the screw.

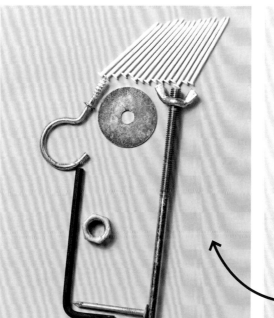

Hardware Friends

Arrange screws and other hardware, like bolts, hooks, nuts, and washers, to make funny faces. How many different ways can you use the parts in your characters?

flexible forts

Did you know you can attach screws to cardboard to make a one-of-a-kind fort? You can make your fort bigger, taller, or more complex by adding more screwed-together walls. These structures can be assembled and then disassembled for storage.

FIND THIS STUFF

Big cardboard boxes or a bunch of little ones | Tape | Corner braces, straight braces, machine screws, washers, and nuts that all fit together | Pencil | Awl | Hot glue gun | Small wrench

GET STARTED

1. Take a look at the cardboard you have to work with. Large pieces can be used for walls. You can tape smaller pieces together to make walls, too. Scraps can be used for roof tiles or trim.

2. Use L-shaped corner braces to secure the corners of your fort. With a pencil, mark the place on the cardboard where each brace will go. Using an awl, poke a hole in the cardboard where each screw will go. Then glue a washer around each hole for strength. Attach the walls together with screws and nuts and tighten with a wrench.

3. Use straight braces to secure cardboard pieces that extend your walls, like if you're adding a tall turret. Mark the location of each straight brace, poke holes where its screws will go, glue a washer over each hole, and then secure the walls with screws and nuts.

PLAY & EXPLORE

Once you have a structure that you feel comfortable going inside, you can start making it your own. Add a cardboard roof, trim the top to look like a cottage or a castle, or both!

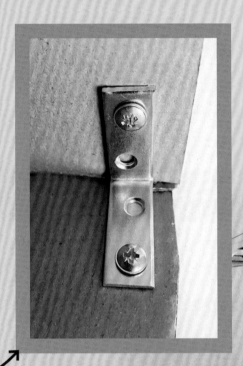

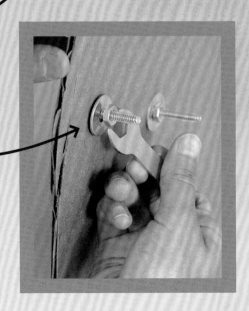

Can you add extra rooms to your fort? How about a sunroom with a higher ceiling?

If you build tall, you might have to make structural supports. Long skinny boxes or poster tubes taped between the two pieces can provide some stability.

Cut out cardboard doors and windows. Use hinges to secure them so they open and close.

Make a circular porthole by cutting an X shape, then making a circle with your utility knife. Make a ring of cardboard and fit it in the hole.

You can use metallic tape, markers, fabric, or other materials to decorate the outside of your fort. Inside you can put blankets, pillows, and fairy lights.

GO DEEPER ↓

GOING DEEPER

freestyle forts

Explore the world of tinkering with large-scale structures that you can go inside. From tree houses to blanket forts, the possibilities are endless.

Three-Sided Hideaway

One simple way that you can construct a fort is by connecting three large pieces of cardboard with right angles. Hang a blanket over the top and enjoy your hideout. Here's a little model of a three-sided fort.

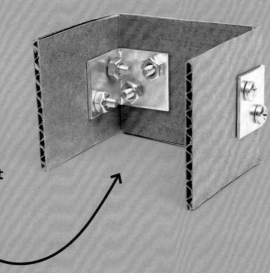

Wooden Fort

With more time, space, and perhaps the help of an adult, you can build an outdoor wooden fort or even a tree house with branches or wood scraps. Start from the ground and work up, be sure to secure the corners, and test the fort's strength and stability.

S·T·E·A·M Connections
ANGLES

Do you notice that your cardboard fort is more stable when the corners are at 90-degree angles? A 90-degree angle, also known as a right angle, directs the force from the walls straight down to the ground. If the angle is smaller (acute), you risk the fort crumpling from the inside. If the angle is wider (obtuse), the structure might slip out on the edges. But, of course, there are exceptions to every rule. As you build, experiment with which angles provide the best support for different structures, and tinker with ways to reinforce your corners.

Extra Hardware

Install a chain or deadbolt on your fort's door to lock it from the inside.

Take Apart & Build New Forts

The pieces in the cardboard fort can be disassembled and reassembled. Try reorganizing the sides to change the location of the door or windows. Use the pieces you made to construct new fort designs.

Doorbells & Chimes

If you know how to wire an electrical circuit (see page 28), you can add a working doorbell or lights to your fort. See if you can scrounge up an old doorbell or chimes to add a bit of real-life charm to your structure.

BEARING BALLS & MARBLES

Bearing balls are made of metal. They are designed to be used in ball bearings—mechanical joints that allow machine parts to turn or slide—but are also used in other industrial applications as well as toys, games, and ball runs. Marbles are made out of glass, metal, or ceramic. You can find bearings at a hardware store and cool marbles at a garage sale, or you can order both online.

HOW ARE THEY MADE?

The process used to make bearing balls is fascinating. They start out as a length of metal wire. The wire is cut into pieces approximately the diameter of the balls. They are pressed into a rough circle, filed down, grinded, heated, grinded again, and then lapped, which is a process that gives the balls their smooth, shiny finish.

What can you do with BEARING BALLS & MARBLES right now?

Spinning Top

Experiment with making a top out of bearing balls and clay. How can you change the number or arrangement of the balls so that the top can be more stable and spin longer?

Rolling Art

Create art by dipping a ball or marble in tempera paint and rolling it across white paper. Experiment with different sizes of bearing balls and marbles and various colors of paint.

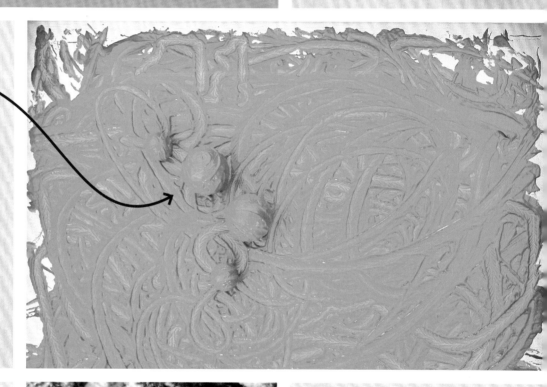

Eye See You!

Use the balls or marbles for eyes on a wooden or cardboard sculpture to create a slightly eerie face.

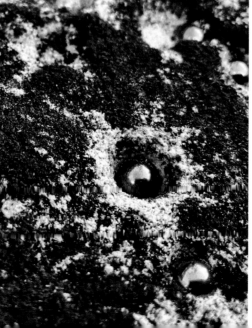

Deep Impact!

Drop a bearing ball in a pile of flour, cinnamon, or other sandy/powdery material. Notice the impact crater and pattern. How does changing the height of the drop change the way the impact surface looks?

chair marble run

How slowly can you get a bearing ball or marble to travel from the top to the bottom of a chair? The path you build for the ball to roll down can be as simple or complicated as you like.

FIND THIS STUFF

Chair | Masking tape | Cardboard, paper-towel tubes, wood molding tracks, plastic tubes, funnels, and any other material you want to experiment with | Marbles or bearing balls

GET STARTED

1. Pick out a chair with hard surfaces that you can use to build your marble run. If the back is curved, you can tape a sheet of cardboard to the back to make a flat surface.

2. Tape a paper-towel tube across the top of the chair. Send a marble down to test if it rolls.

3. Add pieces of wooden track, tubes, funnels, or other materials, creating a pathway for the marble to slowly travel down the chair.

PLAY & EXPLORE

Start your marble run above the top of the chair. You can tape a funnel at the starting point if you like.

Wooden blocks or recycled boxes can be important to stop the ball and redirect it into the next part of the machine.

Tape helps! Don't be afraid to use a lot of tape on your marble run to keep everything in place.

Use all the sides and the back of the chair so there's a longer path for the marble to slowly roll down.

Get a bowl or cup and fill it with marbles or bearing balls. Put it next to your chair so that you can test often. Try another marble or ball each time you add something to your creation.

Hang a track suspended underneath the chair with tape or pipe cleaners.

Connect tubes or boxes to your chair to add structural support to your tracks.

Add a finale to the end of your machine to celebrate the marble reaching the bottom of the track.

GO DEEPER ↓

GOING DEEPER

more marble mazes

How many ways can a marble or bearing ball travel down a path? Build mazes out of cardboard, wood, snow, or recycled materials.

Winter Run

Do you have a snowy hill that can be sculpted into curves and tracks? Make an outdoor run on a snowy day.

Tell a Story

Use some paper and cardboard construction decorations to add bits of narrative to your maze. For example, you could add paper gnomes around your track to tell a story of transporting round emeralds from a cave to a village.

Cardboard Mini Maze

Get a shallow cardboard box and several small strips of cardboard, and construct a cardboard maze. You can make a start and a finish as well as little holes for the ball to fall through when it goes down the wrong path.

Nature Run

Create a marble run using the landscape of the natural world. You can go out to a trail, a playground, or a beach with wood scraps, dowels, cups, and marbles. Tinkerer **Liam Nilsen** explores the idea of a "flexible and irregular surface without walls limiting the boundaries of the exploration."

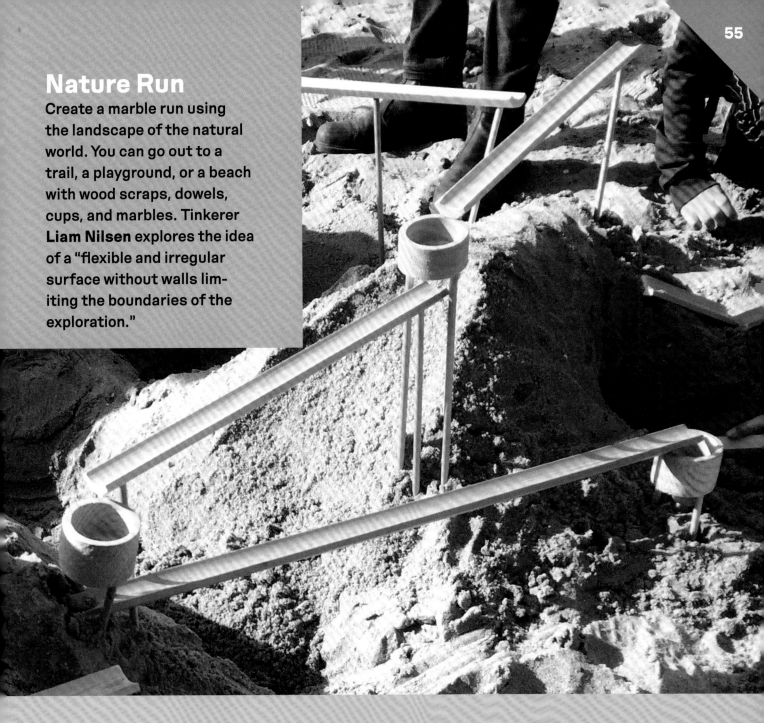

S·T·E·A·M Connections
PROBABILITY

When you build and test marble machines, you are exploring the idea of probability. This means observing how often the marble reaches the destination. If you send a marble down 10 times and it works 5 times, your machine has a 50 percent success rate. Make a change to your machine, and then try sending another 10 marbles down to see how many times they get to the end. Did your change make it more or less probable that the marble will reach the destination?

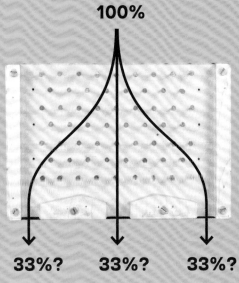

100%

33%? 33%? 33%?

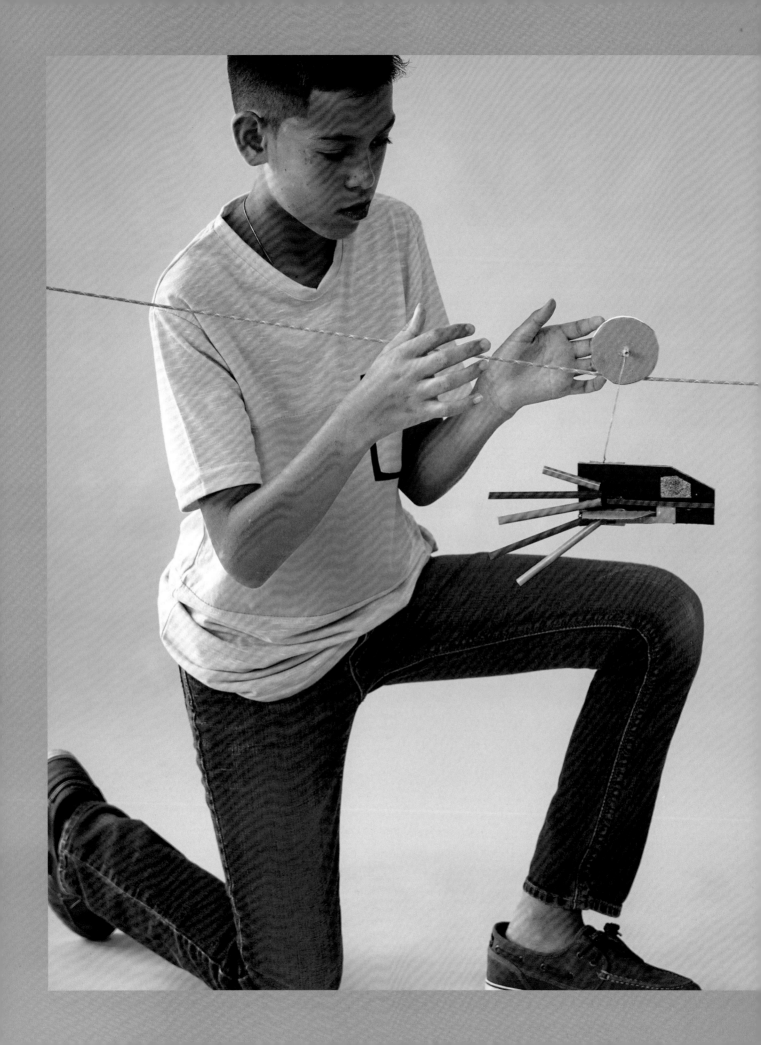

CHAPTER 3
balance

What happens when you train a wire creature to balance on your finger, suspend a set of rainbow-colored shapes from a single point, or propel a cable car on a string across two buildings?

WASHERS

Washers are disks of metal with holes in the middle. They have a practical use for protecting a base material when you're attaching a screw or bolt. Washers can also keep shaking and vibrating things from coming apart. They can be used in all sorts of interesting ways because of their doughnut shape. You can buy washers of all sizes and many different materials at the hardware store.

WHAT DO THE NUMBERS MEAN?

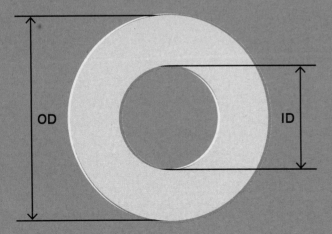

OD

ID

When you are looking for washers, you will often see them listed with two numbers, labeled ID and OD. These stand for the **inner diameter (ID)**, or length across the center of the hole, and the **outer diameter (OD)**, which is the length across the entire ring of metal.

What can you do with
WASHERS
right now?

Draw Circles

Trace the outside or inside of a washer with colored pencil or thin marker to make perfect circles. Can you use a washer as a template for a hand-drawn googly eye?

Make a Game

Attach an open cup to the inside of a box. Stand back and start tossing washers. You get one point for tossing a washer into the box and two points for getting it in the cup.

Roll Away!

Grab a handful of washers and toss them so they roll on their edges. See how far they will go. Observe how different weights and thicknesses make them more or less stable.

Spinning Wheel

Set a washer on its edge and flick one side with your finger to start it turning. How long can it spin?

Weighted Wobblers

Adding washer weights to wire can help you explore balance and stability. Build a sculpture that stays perched on a single point—a pencil eraser!

FIND THIS STUFF

Jar | Washers of different sizes | Rice or lentils (optional) | Masking tape | Pencil | Safety goggles | Round-nose pliers | Roll of 18-gauge stainless steel wire | Decorations

GET STARTED

1. Make a base for your wobbler by filling a jar with washers (or rice or lentils) so it's heavy. Tape a pencil to the side with the eraser pointing up.

2. Wearing safety googles and using the pliers, cut a piece of wire. Bend it into an M shape. Can you balance it on the eraser using the middle point?

3. Add weight to the ends of the wire by bending them into hooks and threading on washers.

4. Add decorations to your design to make it come to life! As you add elements, your sculpture might fall out of balance. Just add, remove, or adjust parts until you are satisified with the results.

PLAY & EXPLORE

There's more than one way to arrange your wobbler. Try bending the wire in new ways or adding new design elements.

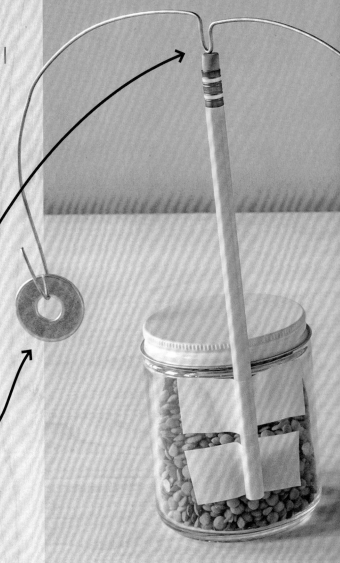

Look closely at the place where the wobbler is balanced. Is it stable or wobbly? What happens if you change the shape or size of the balancing point?

Build above the balancing point.

If your sculpture tilts too far to one side, try adding or subtracting washers, or try bending the wire closer to or farther from the center point.

What happens when you add extra washers or pipe cleaners on the ends of the wires?

GO DEEPER ↓

GOING DEEPER

balancing acts

How many different kinds of wobblers can you make? Try these new ways to play and explore your own designs for kinetic sculptures.

Heavy Weight

Go more extreme with light and heavy weights. Would it be possible to build a wobbler sculpture with an old hiking boot on one side and a goose feather on the other?

Windy Wobbler

Place your creation outside on a windy day or inside near a fan. Watch how the moving air makes the sculpture move and spin. Can you change something in your sculpture to make it move faster or slower?

Material Swap

Test out different materials for your balancing sculpture. Try poking toothpicks through cardboard to make slide-able balance blocks. For the balancing point, try replacing the pencil with a clothespin, a scrap of wood, or even your thumb. Which materials make stable sculptures?

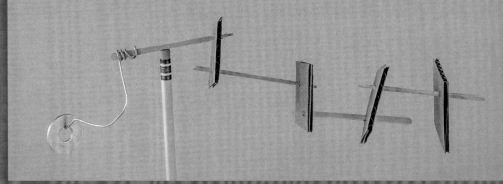

S·T·E·A·M Connections
BALANCE

Dynamic balance is the ability of something to stay standing or stable as it moves. Think about a seesaw on a playground with two kids who are the same weight. If they didn't move, they would both be balanced and up in the air, but because they shift their weight by moving their arms and legs back and forth, the seesaw tilts up and down.

The same thing is happening with your wobbly sculptures. Things in the environment, like the wind or vibrations on your building surface, push the structure in and out of balance. You can play with dynamic balance by having materials on your sculpture that catch the breeze.

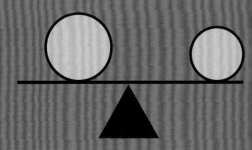

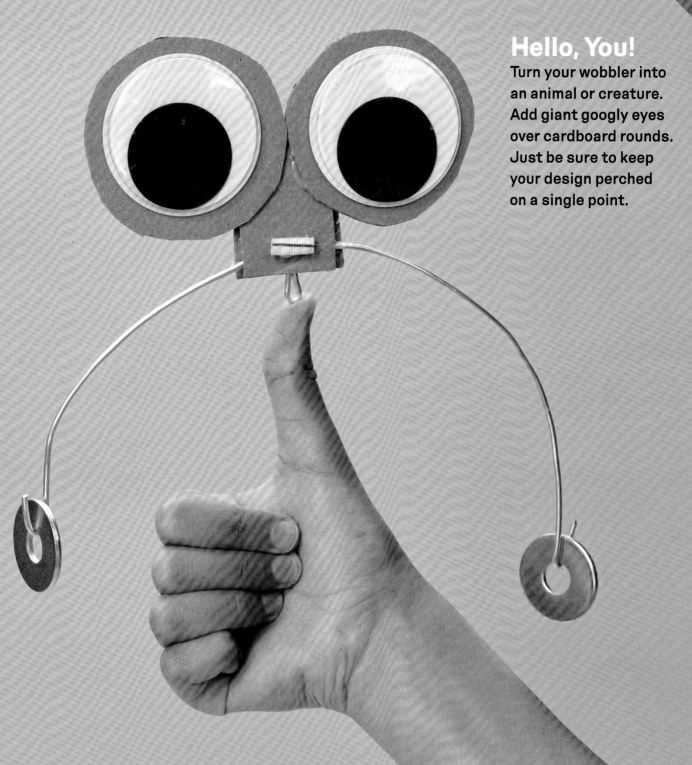

Hello, You!

Turn your wobbler into an animal or creature. Add giant googly eyes over cardboard rounds. Just be sure to keep your design perched on a single point.

Body Balancer

For a fun challenge, build something that can balance on your body. You could give a thumbs up and have a little balancing point. Can you stand on one leg and balance the sculpture on your shoe? How do you have to move to keep the kinetic sculpture in balance?

STAINLESS STEEL WIRE

Stainless steel wire is strong but easy to work with and can be bent in all kinds of shapes. This type of wire can be used for sculptural or mechanical elements for tinkering projects. You can find wire on the shelves of hardware stores. Unbending a paper clip is another easy way to get a little bit of useful wire. You can always reuse your scraps by straightening them out again.

10 12 14 16 18 20 22 24 26 28

WHAT DO THE NUMBERS MEAN?

Wire comes in different thicknesses, which is called the gauge of the wire. The lower the number, the thicker the wire. A 10-gauge wire can be used to make solid structures and a 24-gauge wire is better for delicate work. For the tinkering projects in this book, a 16- or 18-gauge wire is a good place to start.

What can you do with WIRE right now?

Wire Shapes

Use your hands or small pliers to shape wire. It's fun to practice creating different shapes and designs. You can try bending the wire into a circle, square, or star. Twist a wire around a pencil to make a spring. See the difference between a tight and loose spiral?

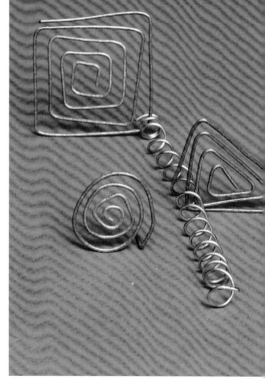

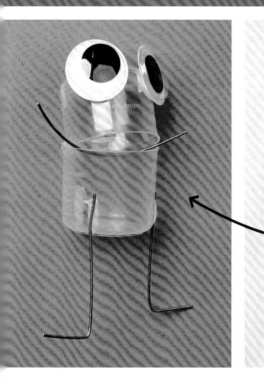

Wire Zoo!

Grab some recycled cups and googly eyes. Attach wire and bend the pieces into the shape of the arms, legs, and head of an animal. You could get inspired to make an entire wire zoo or circus.

Wire Chain

Cut little pieces of wire a few inches long. Bend each into a small circle that's almost closed. Connect two together and close the gap. Add more to make a chain.

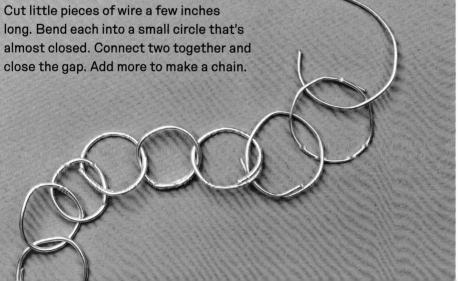

Make Jewelry

Bend the wire into a beautiful shape and create a necklace or bracelet. Explore circuitry (see page 28) and add LEDs to your wearable wire designs.

wire mobiles

Build a twisting, turning, tilting mobile with colorful shapes that move in the breeze. Mobiles bring in elements of science and art, and sometimes it's hard to tell the boundaries between the two.

FIND THIS STUFF

Scissors | Cardboard | Glue | Colored paper or stickers | Safety goggles | Round-nose pliers | Roll of 16- or 18-gauge stainless steel wire | Black marker

GET STARTED

1. Cut out several cardboard shapes and glue on colored paper or decorate with stickers. Wearing safety goggles and using the pliers, snip several pieces of wire between 6 and 12 inches long.

2. Poke one of the cardboard shapes onto each end of one of the wire pieces.

3. Use your finger to find the place where the two shapes are in balance. Mark that point with a marker.

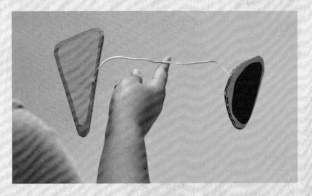

4. Use the pliers to bend a small loop at your mark. Test it to make sure you can still balance the wire with your finger under the loop.

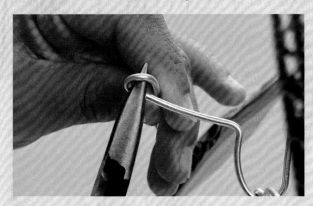

5. Get another piece of wire. Add a U-shaped hook on one end and a cardboard shape on the other. Place the hook through the loop you made in step 4. Now find the balance point on the second piece of wire, mark it, and make another loop.

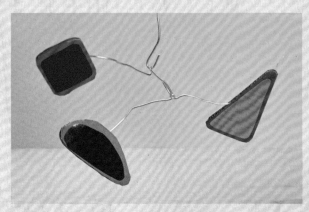

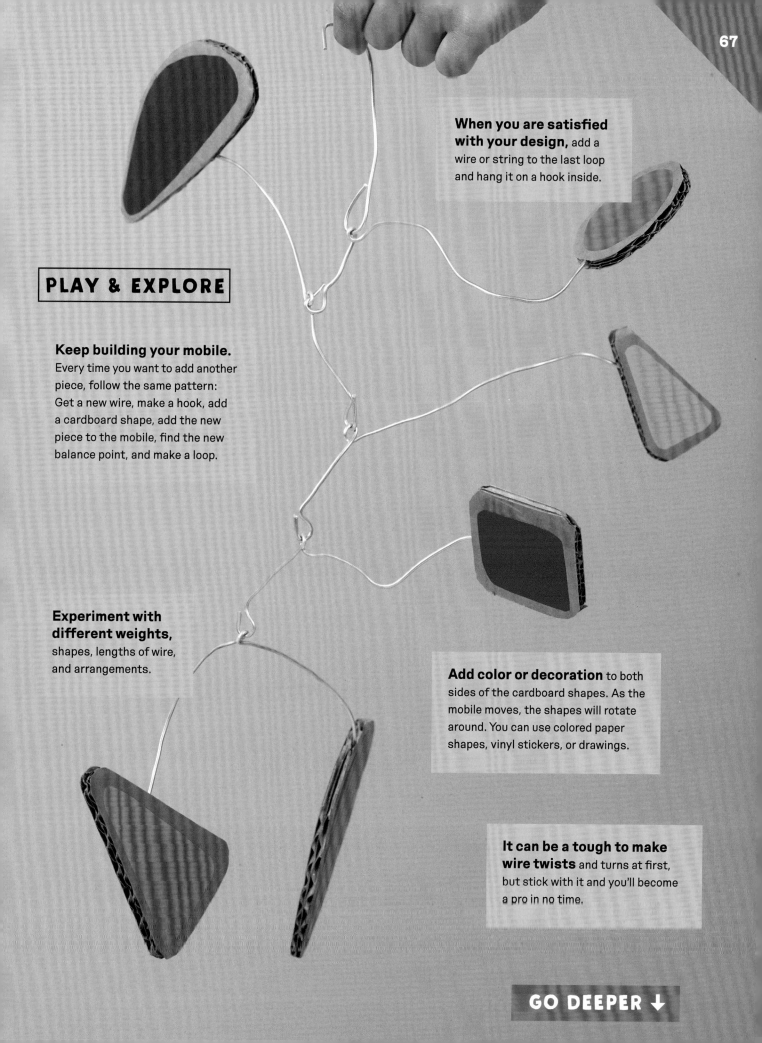

When you are satisfied with your design, add a wire or string to the last loop and hang it on a hook inside.

PLAY & EXPLORE

Keep building your mobile. Every time you want to add another piece, follow the same pattern: Get a new wire, make a hook, add a cardboard shape, add the new piece to the mobile, find the new balance point, and make a loop.

Experiment with different weights, shapes, lengths of wire, and arrangements.

Add color or decoration to both sides of the cardboard shapes. As the mobile moves, the shapes will rotate around. You can use colored paper shapes, vinyl stickers, or drawings.

It can be a tough to make wire twists and turns at first, but stick with it and you'll become a pro in no time.

GO DEEPER ↓

GOING DEEPER

hang in there

As you work on more mobiles, experiment with shapes and materials that look interesting and are fun to build with.

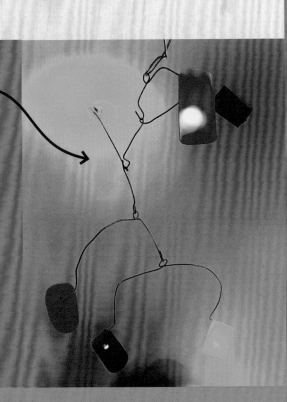

Glowing Mobile

Add LEDs to make your mobile glow at night. You can construct paper or fabric lanterns that diffuse the light in your hanging creations.

Play with Size & Scale

Can you make a tiny mobile that hangs down in a small space? What other shapes and sizes of mobiles can you make?

S·T·E·A·M Connections
TORQUE

Each time you add another piece to your mobile, you can observe the effects of torque on the balancing sculpture. Torque is the tendency for a force to turn or twist. This happens when a heavy object close to the center balances with a lighter object farther away. When you play with the weights of the hanging objects in your mobile and the distance to the balancing point, you see the effect of torque as the mobile rotates, jumps up, twists, and turns.

Hanging Story

Tell a story across hanging panels, like a comic book suspended in the air. You could build a family tree with photos of different family members. Or cut out letters so that the mobile spells out your name.

Recycled Mobile Material

Try making a mobile with recycled colorful cups and spoons. An ice cream parlor might be a good place to get supplies. Experiment with new ways to connect the elements with wire.

STRING & ROPE

String is a long flexible material made from fibers. Rope is made from multiple strings that are twisted together. String and rope can be used for many different projects, from toys to instruments to tools. You can find string and rope at the hardware store. Thinner string can be found at craft supply or fabric stores or online. In your tinkering projects, you might use sewing thread, kite string, fishing line, paracord, twine, or cotton rope, which all have different thicknesses and strengths.

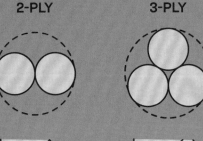

2-PLY   **3-PLY**

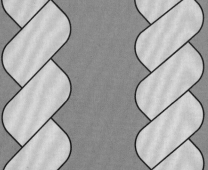

WHAT DO THE NUMBERS MEAN?

When you buy rope (or yarn or twine), the package may say two-ply or three-ply. The number tells you how many strings are in the rope. Rope with three strings is stronger and smoother than rope with two strings.

What can you do with STRING & ROPE right now?

Bubble Blower

Secure a loop of string, with one washer strung onto it, between two dowels. Dip the string in bubble solution, then slowly walk backward with the dowels held in front of you. When the bubble is big enough, start to close the string loop by moving the dowels together.

Make String Art

Grab a piece of scrap wood and mark the perimeter of a square, pentagon, or hexagon with a pencil. Hammer in nails at the corners, then hammer in more nails around the perimeter, spacing them evenly and leaving them all poking up about an inch from the wood. Wrap string around the nails to make beautiful geometric designs.

sky trams

Build balancing tram cars and send them across a long length of rope. Your tram could look like a bus, a spaceship, or a character—the sky's the limit. They can be used to carry secret messages or to transport objects over areas that are hard to get across.

FIND THIS STUFF

Long piece of string | 2 chairs | Plastic spool | Hot glue gun | Cardboard | Awl | Straw | Safety goggles | Length of 18-gauge stainless steel wire | Homemade tram car (made with cardboard and straws, like the one pictured on the facing page)

GET STARTED

1. Tie a piece of string between two chairs. Give your line a slight slope.

2. Take your plastic spool and glue a circle of cardboard over each end. With an awl, poke a hole in the center of the cardboard just big enough for your straw to fit snugly.

3. Push the straw through the hole so it extends out on either end of the spool. Add a bit of glue on the outside of the straw so it stays in place. Wearing safety goggles, cut a long piece of wire and thread it through the straw. The wheel should spin smoothly on the wire. Bend the end of the wire so it can't slip out.

4. Glue the other end of the wire to a homemade tram car, bending the wire so that the tram dangles under the spinning spool. Bend the wires and adjust the tram car so that it balances and moves down the line.

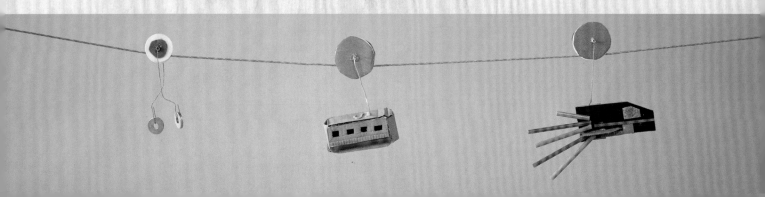

PLAY & EXPLORE

Hold the tram and flick the wheel to see how well it spins.

Set the spool on the line, give your sky tram a push, and see how it moves. You can change the angle of the string to make it roll as you like.

How slowly can you make your tram travel down the string?

Think of a theme and deck out your vehicle. It could be designed to look a gondola or like an alien-filled commuter bus. As you add elements to the tram car, keep testing to make sure it stays stable on the line.

Adjust the wire so the tram balances just under the line. You'll need to make small tweaks to the wire position.

Add weight, such as washers or nuts, on the bottom of the sky tram so that gravity helps it stay on the line (but not so much weight that it has trouble moving!). You can change the number of wheels, the arrangement of the frame, and the style of the weighted part on the bottom.

GO DEEPER ↓

GOING DEEPER

world on a string

Investigate different ways your sky vehicles look and move along the string. Explore new materials and keep fine-tuning your designs.

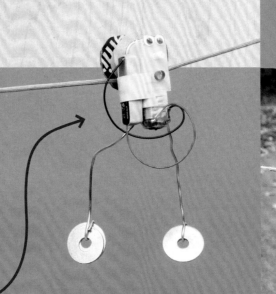

Motorized Tram

Can you make a motorized machine to go **up** the line? You'll have to consider the extra weight of the battery and the motor.

Outdoor Sky Tram

Take your string outside and make your tram travel through nature. Tie the ends to two trees, traffic cones, or railings.

Film It

If you send your sky tram to daring places, take a film of the journey. Figure out how to strap on an old digital camera or camera phone and film the trip down the line.

S·T·E·A·M Connections
FRICTION

The speed at which your creation moves down the line is related to friction, the sticky force that is produced when two materials rub against each other. Friction is affected by the bumps and irregularities in the surface of two materials that come in contact with each other, but it's more complicated than that. The weight of the objects also creates more friction. This can be good to keep in mind when you build your tram. Too much weight and your vehicle won't move; too little and it might fall off the line.

Wheel Away!

If you can't find a spool, you can make your own wheel with plastic cups, bottle caps, or other recyclables.

Toy Tram

Get creative with your tram. How about making one out of a berry basket? Fill it with toy animals, and carry the cargo across the room.

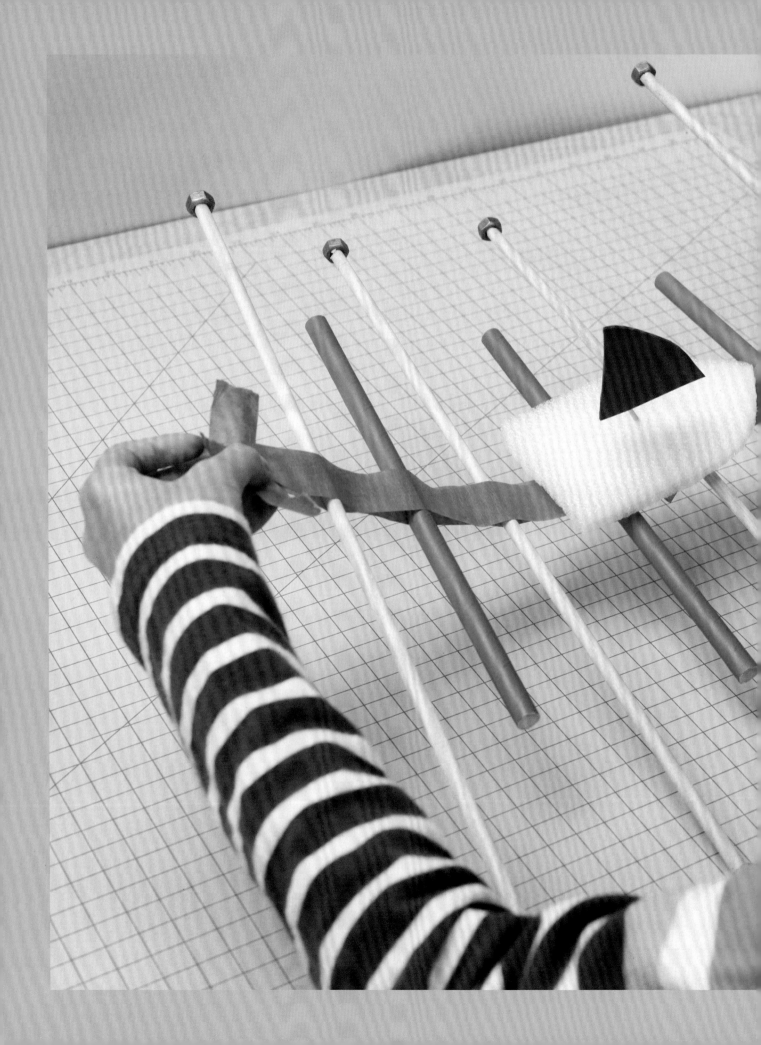

CHAPTER 4
mechanisms

What happens when you turn a
handle to make a character dance,
go fishing with linkages, or rock a
boat on wooden waves?

CARDBOARD

Cardboard sparks imagination. It can become a robot costume, a spaceship, a stovetop, or a secret club hideout. Corrugated cardboard, the stuff that boxes are made of, has two thin sheets of paper on either side of a third wavy sheet. It's easy to find free cardboard. Just save boxes from mail deliveries or ask at supermarkets or furniture stores if they have scrap cardboard. And if your family gets a new refrigerator or washing machine, save that box!

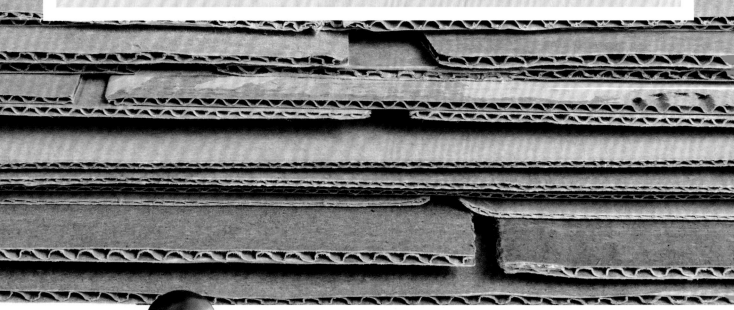

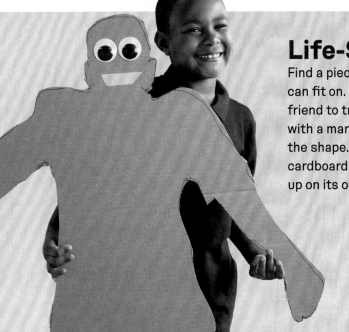

Life-Size Selfie

Find a piece of cardboard you can fit on. Lie on it, and ask a friend to trace around your body with a marker. Then cut out the shape. Can you make your cardboard doppelganger stand up on its own?

Gears

When exposed, the wavy section inside corrugated cardboard can open up possibilities for messing about with cardboard gears. Can you make the ridges fit together and spin?

What can you do with CARDBOARD right now?

Cardboard Costume

Start small with a fuzzy mustache or stylish glasses. Then try building a hat, mask, or suit.

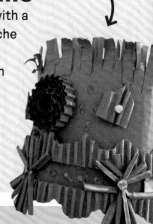

Stalagmites!

Cut a long strip of flexible cardboard. Start twisting the piece, moving down a bit each time. When you get to the end, add a dab of hot glue or tape. Place stalagmites of various shapes and sizes in a dark place like a closet or cellar. Feel free to add cardboard bats and spiders.

Big Face Box

Yuji Hayashi invented this really fun project. Find a cardboard box that fits over your head. Cut a hole in the front. Cover the opening with a Fresnel lens (which you can buy online) and tape it in place. Add a row of white battery-powered lights around the sides of the lens. Put the box over your head and observe the hilarious effects. Try with different types of lenses or colorful or blinking lights. Can you make the big box balance on your shoulders? Have fun experimenting with this magnifying mask!

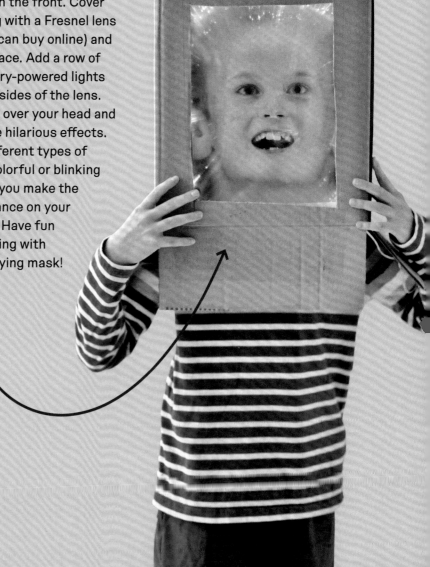

Cardboard Crank Sliders

An automata is a crank-powered toy. It can be built out of different materials. You can make one with just a piece of cardboard and some wire. Try using this basic design to build a range of moving characters.

FIND THIS STUFF

Scissors or utility knife | Sturdy cardboard | Hot glue gun | Safety goggles | Round-nose pliers | 18-gauge stainless steel wire | Craft foam | Masking tape | Colored paper | Googly eyes

GET STARTED

1. Start by building a base. Using scissors or a utility knife, cut out two rectangles and a small right triangle from a piece of cardboard. Arrange the rectangles in an L-shape and hot glue the triangle between the two pieces to form a stable corner.

2. Cut a small rectangle and glue it on the front, as shown.

3. Wearing safety goggles, use pliers to cut three or four pieces of wire, each about 8 to 10 inches long.

4. Slip a piece of wire through the corrugation in the cardboard rectangle on the front of your machine. Bend an **L** on one end for the handle and a **U** on the other end for the crank piece.

5. Cut a foam square and slip it onto the **U** end. Stick one end of another piece of wire into the foam so that the wire stands upright, as shown. On the other end of the wire, use tape to attach a homemade paper flag that moves when the **L** handle is cranked.

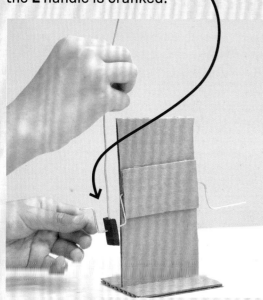

6. A third piece of wire will serve as a limiter—a device that limits the motion of the flag wire, allowing it to move up and down but not from side to side. Bend one end of this third wire into a small loop and run the flag wire through it. Using pliers, snip and bend the other end of the wire so that it can sit behind the upright cardboard piece and hot-glue it in place, as shown.

7. Turn the crank. You should be able to see the flag move up and down. Add a googly eye and a colored paper mouth and hair to make a character.

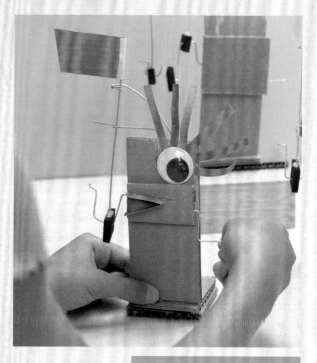

GO DEEPER ↓

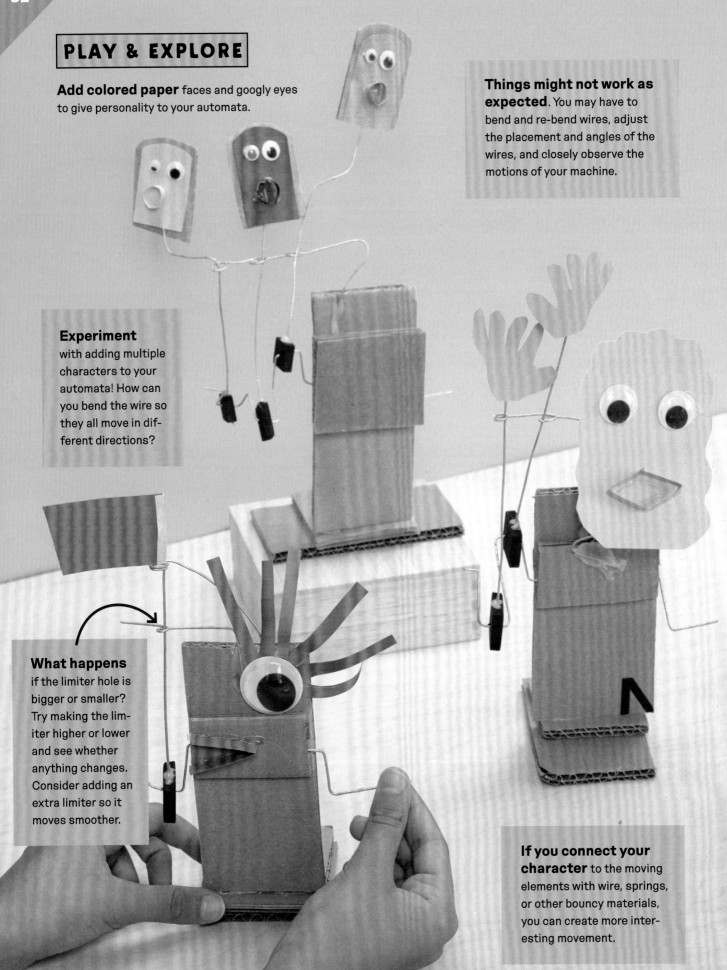

PLAY & EXPLORE

Add colored paper faces and googly eyes to give personality to your automata.

Things might not work as expected. You may have to bend and re-bend wires, adjust the placement and angles of the wires, and closely observe the motions of your machine.

Experiment with adding multiple characters to your automata! How can you bend the wire so they all move in different directions?

What happens if the limiter hole is bigger or smaller? Try making the limiter higher or lower and see whether anything changes. Consider adding an extra limiter so it moves smoother.

If you connect your character to the moving elements with wire, springs, or other bouncy materials, you can create more interesting movement.

keep cranking!

After building an automata with a crank slider, you can imagine the possibilities of multiple animated characters moving up and down and around.

Light Play

Attach colorful pieces of soda bottles or food containers, bubble wrap, mirrors, or plastic crystals to the moving piece. Position your machine in front of a light and behind a white screen and watch the light play.

Storytelling

Ryoko Matsumoto is a museum educator who helped develop this project. She says, "When you are tinkering with cranky contraptions, you are exploring motion, mechanism, and storytelling."

Sound Machine

Notice how the moving element goes back and forth. Attach a jingle bell and make it ring. How else can you use an automata's motion to make noise?

Tinkering Inspiration
SERIOUSLY PLAYFUL

Automata makers are artists, engineers, and tinkerers. **Keith Newstead** used wood, wire, and found materials to build crank-powered machines like this elephant, made from an old detergent bottle.

Automata makers explore mechanical ideas like **levers, cranks, cams, and gears.** But that doesn't stop them from thinking of unexpected ways to use their materials. When you build automata with recycled materials, use your imagination. Engineer your own fun and silly ways to give cardboard boxes, plastic containers, and scrap wood new life.

DOWELS

Dowels are circular rods made from wood or sometimes plastic and metal. Among other uses, carpenters and woodworkers use them for joining together two pieces of wood, as an alternative to screws. They usually come in short 1- or 2-inch pieces or in yard-long rods that can be cut down to size. Wooden dowels can usually be found in the lumber section of the hardware store.

HOW TO FIND THE DIAMETER OF A DOWEL

You can use a dowel plate to test the size of the dowels. Just slip the dowel into the holes of this measuring tool, and when you find the one that fits, read the corresponding number.

If you have a set of drill bits, you can use the case to test-fit your dowels. Or you can make your own dowel plate by drilling holes into a block of wood that are the same size as common dowel diameters.

What can you do with DOWELS right now?

Balance a Dowel

Hold one on its end in the palm of your hand. Can you balance it? Then try adding a heavy weight to the top of the dowel. Does it make the dowel harder or easier to balance?

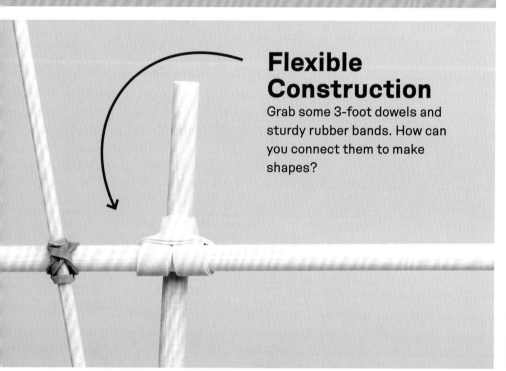

Flexible Construction

Grab some 3-foot dowels and sturdy rubber bands. How can you connect them to make shapes?

Beat It

Use dowels as drumsticks and listen for the different sounds you can make. Taping a bunch of dowels together will create an interesting percussion instrument.

Dowel Rope Sculpture

Another way to build big with dowels is by sticking them into the ground or building a base and connecting them with long pieces of ribbon, rope, or yarn.

making waves

Experiment with dowels and straws to create this playful wave machine. Once it is set up, just shake a dowel and watch your wave move. You can play with size and scale and even rock a boat on your wave.

FIND THIS STUFF

Blue painter's tape | 20 to 30 ¼-inch-diameter wooden dowels about 12 inches long | Straws | 2 chairs

PLAY & EXPLORE

Try different ways of playing with your wave. You can gently move it up and down or give it a strong shake. Can you send a wave back and forth? Can you push and pull the structure so that it makes a standing wave?

Add a boat, ocean birds, or a sea monster to your scene. Can you make the waves animate your designs?

GET STARTED

1. Lay a long length of blue painter's tape on a table with the sticky side facing up.

2. Place the dowels on the tape so that they are roughly an equal distance from each other. If you want, you can alternate dowels with straws. Add a second strip of tape on top of dowels to hold them in place.

3. Suspend the wave between two chairs or sturdy anchors. Use plenty of tape to firmly attach the ends to the chairs.

4. Gently rock a dowel and watch your wave move back and forth.

Test out how taut the strip of dowels needs to be by tightening or loosening the connection at the ends of the wave, or moving the chairs.

You may need to adjust the placement of the sticks and the width of the tape to make sure that each of the dowels can move freely.

Experiment by adding nuts or washers as weights on the ends of the dowels. Use tape or glue to securely attach your weights.

GO DEEPER ↓

GOING DEEPER

Catch a wave!

Discover ways to trigger your wave machine with motors, change its size and scale, and make an interesting story.

Tiny Waves

Experiment with size and scale. Can you make a tiny wave machine with toothpicks and dowels?

Wiffle Ball Waves

Go a bit more 3-D with your design. Try to connect Wiffle balls together with string and hang them from a structure made of dowels or PVC pipe. What other kinds of pattern machines can you make?

Glow in the Dark

Use little LED throwies as weights on the ends of the wave machine dowels for a glow-in-the-dark experiment. (See page 131 for directions on how to make a throwie, a little light-up element with an LED.)

S·T·E·A·M Connections
ACTION-REACTION

According to the laws of physics, when an object moves another object, there's a second reaction that is equal in force but in the opposite direction. As a simple real-world example of action and reaction, when a skateboarder pushes their foot against the ground, the ground "pushes back," causing the skateboard to move forward. When you give your wave machine a push, you trigger a series of actions and reactions.

Artists, engineers, and tinkerers closely observe the movements of their machines to get a sense of how the forces operating on them can be used to make something more useful, beautiful, or fun.

Motor Machine

Use a motor to trigger a wave machine at a steady rate. You could attach one end of a string to your wave machine and the other end to a moving hub so that the string gets regular pulses.

Sail Away!
To make a little boat that travels along your wave, cut a piece of foam or other light material, add a tooth-pick mast, and attach a paper or cloth sail.

BRASS PAPER FASTENERS

Brass fasteners create moving joints in paper and cardboard. The fasteners, also known as brads, have round heads and two legs with points on the ends. Stick the legs through a hole in a stack of papers and then bend them to hold the pages together. This keeps the pages in place but allows them to rotate. Brass fasteners are just one of the many tinkering materials you can find in an office supply store.

WHY ARE THEY MADE OF BRASS?

Brass is a soft and shiny metal that's a mix of copper and zinc. It's used for locks, gears, zippers, and many musical instruments. Brass doesn't rust, it can withstand variable temperatures, and it looks beautiful.

What can you do with
BRASS PAPER
FASTENERS
right now?

3-D Connectors

Instead of paper, try using brass fasteners to connect pieces of toilet paper tubes, the sides of plastic bottles, or egg carton pieces.

Shaker Instrument

Put the brads in a container and shake, shake, shake! Experiment with different materials for the container and see how the sound changes.

Make a Top

Use the round head of a fastener as the point that the top spins on. Stack it with washers, pieces of cardboard, or other materials. Can you find a way to easily spin the top?

MAKE HOLES FOR BRADS

You can use an awl to make a hole in a piece of cardboard where you want to place a brass fastener. Put your cardboard on a stable base made of a piece of foam glued to a wooden block. Hold the cardboard with your other hand a little bit away from where you want to make a hole, line the awl up straight, and press down firmly through the cardboard and into the foam base.

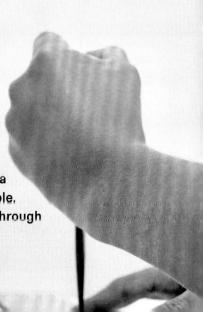

linkage party

What do a bicycle and a hungry eel have in common? They both use linkages to move! You can explore these mechanical connections with cardboard, paper, and brass paper fasteners.

FIND THIS STUFF

Scissors or utility knife | Cardboard | Awl | Brass paper fasteners, at least ½ inch long

GET STARTED

1. Using scissors or a utility knife, cut 4 strips of cardboard that are about 2 inches wide and 12 inches long.

2. To create a four-bar linkage, first use an awl to punch a hole in the center of each strip. Arrange two strips into an X shape and secure them with a fastener pushed through their center holes. Repeat with the remaining two strips so that you have two Xs.

3. Line up the two X shapes so that their ends overlap, as shown. Punch a hole in each spot that overlaps, and place a fastener through those holes. Play with the machine and see how the parts move.

PLAY & EXPLORE

Can you make a fish?
Start with the four-bar linkage from step 2. Rearrange the brads and strips so it looks like the green highlighted part in the diagram below. Add more cardboard strips (shown in tan) to make a fish. Change and customize the pieces for different results.

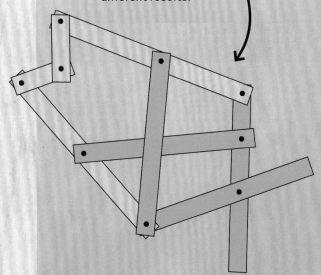

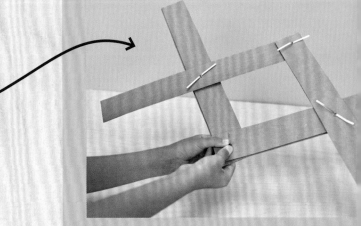

As you play around, think about using linkages to create a character or tell a story. One idea is a fish and a fishing pole with a little rubber-band worm. Add a giant googly eye to the big fish.

Experiment with changing the length of the four bars. You might even have them extend past the corners where they're fastened together.

Move the two ends apart and together again. Notice the way the shape bends and changes.

Have a friend or sibling who also wants to tinker? Make your linkage big enough for the two of you to play together. You may have to invent a way to keep longer cardboard pieces sturdy.

GO DEEPER ↓

mix-and-match mechanisms

Keep exploring the properties of linkages as you make art, design toys, and motorize your creations.

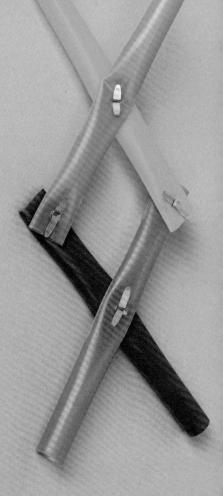

Add Motors

You can add circuits to linkages for more advanced designs. Making connections between electronic circuits and moving cardboard constructions is the foundation for more advanced mechanisms.

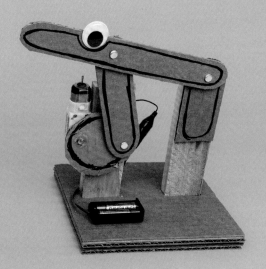

Linkages with Different Materials

Try using plastic straws, metal (think Erector sets), or even LEGO Technic beams.

S·T·E·A·M Connections
SCALE DRAWINGS

Linkages can be used in art to make geometric patterns or change the size and scale of a drawing. If you arrange the mechanisms in the right way, you can draw on one sheet of paper and make the exact same movements, bigger or smaller, on another sheet. This can be a fun project to experiment with. Secure a marker, crayon, or paintbrush dipped in paint at the end of your linkage. Try to turn it into a drawing tool. What sort of masterpieces can you create?

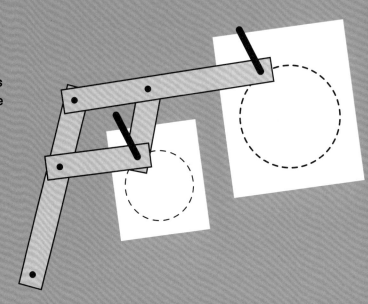

Roller Toy

Make a rolling toy with linkage elements. Look at wooden roller toys designed for babies, where the wheels make some other part of the toy move. These toys are made with linkages, and you can experiment by either hacking an existing toy or making your own from scratch.

Tinkering Inspiration:
LINKAGES WITH CHARACTER

Artist **Noga Elhassid** leads the Moving Toys Workshop for kids. She creates moving cardboard characters that take linkages in all sorts of inspiring directions. She says, "I use cardboard and copper brads because they are easily formed and enable deep explorations in a short time." Noga's creations show playfulness in art and science experiments. She starts with science and engineering and infuses them with color, character, and personality.

CHAPTER 5
light & shadow

What happens when you imagine wonderful worlds hiding in the shadows, map out a kaleidoscopic scavenger hunt in your neighborhood, or catch rays of sunlight with a colorful plastic quilt?

GOOGLY EYES

Googly eyes make people laugh and can turn almost anything into a playful character. Googly eyes are made of white paper, a black circle, and a clear plastic dome that holds the pieces together. The black part of the eye wiggles. Googly eyes can be stuck to paper, cardboard, or plastic with a piece of tape or a dab of hot glue. You can buy them online or at craft stores, or you can make your own.

MAGNETIZE YOUR EYES

Evil Mad Scientist Labs adds magnets on the back of googly eyes so that they can be stuck and restuck to any metallic surface. To make these reusable decorations, cut small pieces from a rubber-backed magnet sheet using scissors. Stick the magnets to the back of your googly eyes with hot glue, and then you can attach them to metal surfaces over and over again.

What can you do with GOOGLY EYES right now?

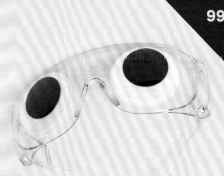

Googly Goggles

Find or make two giant googly eyes. Tape them on your safety glasses or stick one on your forehead. Take a selfie!

Tool Face

Attach googly eyes to a hammer or other tool in your house. Or add them to fruits and veggies in your kitchen. Where can you put the eyes to create the funniest effect?

Hand Puppet

Put a googly eye on your hand to make simple character that can look happy, sad, or angry.

Eye Bomb!

Go out and about and secretly plant googly eyes on everyday objects. This type of street art brings laughs to passersby. You'll need some magnetic googly eyes or regular eyes and masking tape. Take photos of your art!

Here's an example made by artist **Jode Roberts**.

shadow scenes

Have you ever looked up at the clouds and imagined you saw something like a pig, a pineapple, or a pirate ship? In this project, you can create shadows on the wall and use your imagination in a similar way. Arrange objects, cast a light to make shadows, and look for silly faces, aliens, or monsters!

FIND THIS STUFF

Large sheet of white paper | Masking tape | Objects that cast interesting shadows, such as hand tools, kitchen supplies, hardware store treasures, or natural objects | Flashlight with the lens unscrewed, or cell phone light | Googly eyes | Markers

GET STARTED

1. Attach a big sheet of white paper to a wall with masking tape.

2. Arrange your objects on a table, darken the room, and shine your light to cast a shadow on the paper.

3. What do you see? Does the shadow look like a face, an animal, a monster, or an alien?

4. Place googly eyes around the shadows and add drawings and speech bubbles to make a fun character or scene.

PLAY & EXPLORE

Try bringing your objects closer to and farther away from the light. Can you make the shadows bigger or smaller?

Share your ideas by taking a photo of the shadow.

Ask a friend what they see in the shadows.

Build holders for your lights and objects with clothespins, scrap wood, rubber bands, clamps, or a mini camera tripod.

What new shapes and shades emerge when shadows overlap?

Experiment with bigger or smaller googly eyes. You can even make a character with mismatched eyes!

Add thought or speech bubbles to tell a story.

Shadow Play

Keep experimenting with light and shadows with new materials and in new places. What new characters and scenes can you invent?

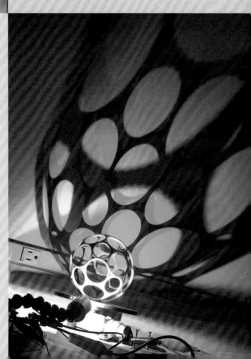

Light Refraction

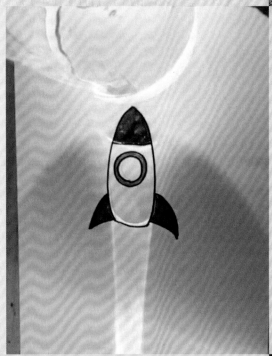

When you shine light through a clear material like glass, plastic, or crystal, it refracts, or bends, with interesting effects. Try using light refraction to create illuminated art that combines light projections and hand-drawn scenes.

Chalk Shadows

Go outside and find or make big shadows. Use chalk and googly eyes to create scenes out of these natural projections. This is a form of public art similar to eye-bombing (see page 99) and can start conversations with passersby.

S·T·E·A·M Connections
SHIFTING SHADOWS

When you play with shadows, you develop an idea about the way they work. You can experiment with how the angle of light affects the way the shadow looks. A shadow from straight-on light looks different than a shadow from light at an angle.

Experiment with all the different ways you can cast a shadow on white paper using just one object and one light source. Then try casting colorful shadows with a red, green, or blue lamp. The small differences in the position of the light source has a big effect on the shadows. Try two or more colored lights, and watch the new colors emerge.

Take Two

Hang a new sheet of paper and experiment with other materials that cast shadows. Take a look at the shadows made by a hairbrush.

Work Backward

Make a drawing with an important part missing, such as a snail without a shell, a butterfly without wings, or a sailboat without a sail. Shine a light and cast a shadow to fill in the missing part of your drawing!

MIRRORS

A mirror is a shiny material that bounces light back into your eyes. Most mirrors are made from glass and metal, but for your tinkering experiments, it's best to use plastic or cardstock with a mirrored surface. These mirrors won't break or shatter, and they can be easily cut into shapes. You can order these types of mirrors online, or you might be able to find them at hardware or home stores. Another fun mirrored material is Mylar, which is a very thin, reflective sheet used for gardening or camping.

Mirror, Mirror

Cover the inside of a bowl completely using small pieces of plastic or cardboard with a mirrored surface. You can use tape or glue to get the little mirrored pieces to stick on. Notice how the bowl reflects light. The inside of a bowl can create some really fun effects!

What can you do with
MIRRORS
right now?

Light Reflection

Attach tiny scraps of mirrors to pieces of wire and create an abstract image on the wall by reflecting the light from the sun or a powerful lamp.

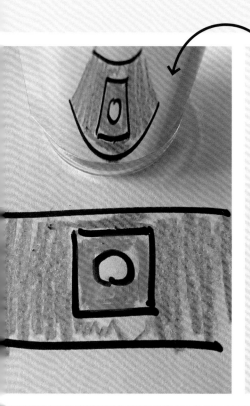

Perspective

Attach a piece of mirrored sheet or Mylar (a reflective material) to a cup with straight sides and put it on a piece of white paper. Explore how drawings you make on the paper appear different when they are reflected in the Mylar.

Rearview Mirror

Use cardboard, wire, and tape to make a wearable rearview mirror so that you can see behind you when you are walking. What do you notice when you look at the world this way?

Cool kaleidoscopes

A kaleidoscope gives you a new way of looking at the world. You can see everyday materials differently, explore color, and discover patterns.

FIND THIS STUFF

Safety goggles | Scissors or utility knife | Mirrored cardstock about 8½ × 11 inches or larger | Scrap cardboard | Masking tape | Cardboard tube

GET STARTED

1. Wearing safety goggles, use scissors or a utility knife to cut three rectangular pieces of mirrored material, each 3 inches long and 1 inch wide. Stick them onto equal-size pieces of cardboard.

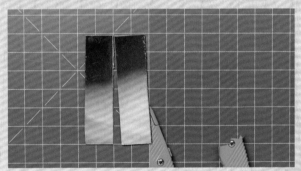

2. Flip them over so the mirror surface faces down. Line them up with just a small gap, about the same width as the material's thickness, between them.

3. Tape over each gap. Fold the pieces together so they form a triangle-shaped box and tape over the last seam, too, to secure it.

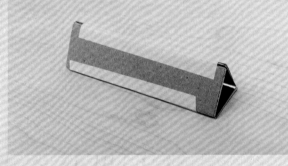

4. Fit the triangle into the cardboard tube. Use more tape, if needed, to hold it in place.

PLAY & EXPLORE

Look through your kaleido-scope at natural objects, like pine cones, small stones, or leaves.

Observe a handful of everyday objects. Try viewing colorful candies, thumbtacks, or a full key ring.

Take your kaleidoscope around your neighborhood and look for interesting things to view.

Search for interesting textures and patterns to view with your scope, like flowers in a garden or geometric wallpaper.

GO DEEPER ↓

new lens on the world

See everyday objects in a new way through your homemade kaleidoscopes!

More Mirrors Kaleidoscope

Experiment with different sizes, numbers, or shapes for the mirrors. What happens when you create a four-sided scope? Does adding more mirrors create more interesting views?

Light Lens

If you want to see larger scenes with a kaleidoscopic pattern, add a convex or spherical lens at the end of your kaleidoscope. You can unscrew the lens on a flashlight or order a clear plastic or glass sphere online. Now when you point your kaleidoscope at buildings, trees, and landscapes, all of the light will be bent toward your eye.

Camera Kaleidoscope

Tape a phone camera to the eyepiece side of the kaleidoscope. Take photos or videos of your discoveries. Share them with family and friends.

S·T·E·A·M Connections
MIRROR MATH

If you want to be more precise with your kaleidoscopes, measure and check the angles with a protractor.

If you are working with two mirrors, you can make a circular reflection by arranging the mirrors at any angle that divides evenly into 360. Some options are 45, 30, or 15 degrees. Does a bigger angle give you larger or smaller reflections? Can you predict how many copies of your image you will see?

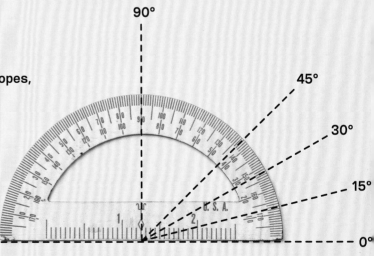

Corner Reflector

Arrange two mirrors next to each other at an angle and tape to make a corner reflector. Bring your angled mirrors outside and look at flowers, grass, and other natural objects.

BUBBLE WRAP

Bubble wrap is made of two sheets of plastic with inflated pillows of air between them. Listen to the different sounds when tiny, quarter-size, and huge bubbles release their air, and notice how much strength you need to pop them. Get free bubble wrap from recycling bins, offices, or your school. Or buy it new at office supply stores, hardware stores, or post offices, or order it online.

KNOW YOUR BUBBLE WRAP

There are many kinds of bubble wrap, with bubbles ranging from about the size of a pinto bean to larger pockets about the size of a quarter and even larger cushions about the size of a hamster. In some bubble wrap all the air pockets are individually sealed, while in others they're connected. You can even find metallic bubble wrap that has shiny foil on either side of a layer of bubble wrap. This metallic bubble wrap is conductive and can be used in electronic explorations.

What can you do with BUBBLE WRAP right now?

Make Prints

The simplest way to try out painting with bubble wrap is by dipping it in paint and pressing it on a sheet of paper. You can also attach a piece to a lint roller and roll on the textured pattern.

Pop 'Em!

If you get stressed out, keep an emergency square of bubble wrap around. Pop the bubbles and relax. There's something soothing about popping the air-filled pockets of bubble wrap until all of the bubbles are flattened.

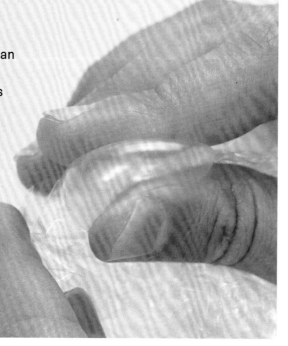

Stomp Shoes

If you want to try a different way to pop bubbles, tape bubble wrap to the bottom of your shoes and see how long it takes to pop them all.

Create Wearables

Have to kneel on the ground for a long time? Make some bubble wrap kneepads!

bubble wrap suncatchers

Smush together sheets of bubble wrap and scraps of recycled plastic with the heat of an iron to make beautiful patterns for sunlight to shine through. You can experiment with the ways in which color, shape, and thickness affect the suncatchers.

FIND THIS STUFF

Scissors | Sheet of bubble wrap | Parchment paper | Colorful plastic bags or plastic scraps | Iron

GET STARTED

1. Using scissors, cut out a piece of bubble wrap and place it on a slightly larger piece of parchment paper. Add scraps of colorful plastic to make a pattern on top of the bubble wrap.

2. Cut out a second piece of parchment paper the same size as the first. Carefully place it on top of your bubble wrap design so that your pattern stays in place.

3. Set the iron temperature for rayon/polyester and place the hot iron on the top layer of parchment paper, pressing gently. Feel the bubbles pop and the plastic start to fuse. Smoothly move your iron over the entire parchment paper surface, making sure the iron doesn't directly touch the plastic.

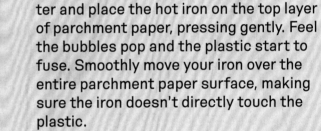

Safety Note: An iron can get very hot. Work with an adult the first time you use one for a tinkering project. Try to work in a place with an open window or good airflow. There can be some slight odors from the fused plastic.

PLAY & EXPLORE

Bring the suncatcher to a window and see the light shine through. How does the pattern change when you look at the suncatcher on a sunny or cloudy day?

Experiment with overlapping multiple layers of bubble wrap with small and large bubbles. What patterns do you notice in the final design?

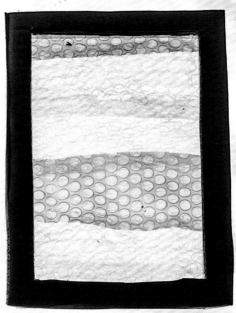

Try out lots of colors and shapes to make different designs. You could make a rainbow pattern or a suncatcher shaped like the leaves of a plant.

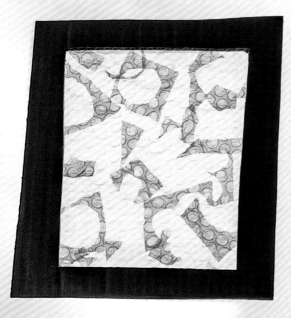

Compare the fused bubble wrap and plastic bags to the original material. How does the light quality change when the material is melted together?

Make a frame out of cardboard for your suncatcher and add string or suction cups so that it can hang in a window.

GO DEEPER ↓

light bubbles

Keep playing with bubble wrap combined with the power of the sun and other light sources. Try new ideas for your fused plastic suncatchers and experiment with other ways to tinker with light.

DIY Designs

Add sewn elements or embroidery stitches to your fused bubble wrap design. You can use thick thread to highlight parts of the design or add more complicated details.

Night-Light

Use cardboard, wire, or wooden dowels to create a three-dimensional frame for your fused bubble wrap piece. Use LEDs to illuminate the inside of your design for a stylish night-light.

S·T·E·A·M Connections
THE SCIENCE OF LIGHT

Light particles are moving all around us in straight lines. When the light hits an object, a few different things can happen. The light can be absorbed, transmitted, or reflected and often it does a combination of those things. If light hits an object like a basketball, some of the light is reflected and some is absorbed. The parts that are reflected go into our eyes and give the object its color and shape. If light hits a clear pane of glass, the light is transmitted, meaning it passes through. If light hits a smooth, shiny surface like a mirror, it is reflected, meaning it bounces off and back to our eyes. Suncatchers look interesting because some light is transmitted, some is reflected, and some is absorbed.

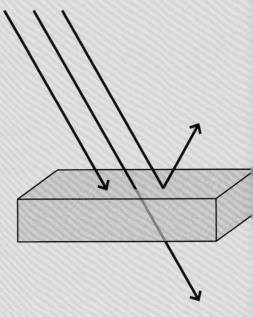

Light Table Art

Find or make a light table where you can prototype your designs before fusing them together. Light tables were originally used for developing film, and you can sometimes find one in a thrift store. To make your own, place LED lights in a clear box with a translucent lid.

Sun Prints

Place bubble wrap on top of sun-print paper or construction paper, leave it out in the sun, and watch the pattern reveal itself over time. If you are using construction paper, it will take longer for the pattern to emerge.

CHAPTER 6
electrical circuits

What happens when you turn a switch
for an instant confetti celebration, use
a robot to create abstract artworks, or
construct a cardboard city that glows
in the dark?

MOTORS

A motor turns electricity into movement. Adding battery-powered motors to tinkering projects can make toys that move, pulleys that lift weights, arms that wave, or bugs that shake. You can order motors online at sites for makers and hobbyists. You can also scavenge motors from battery-powered things. If a moving machine is powered by batteries, the motor can probably be used in tinkering projects.

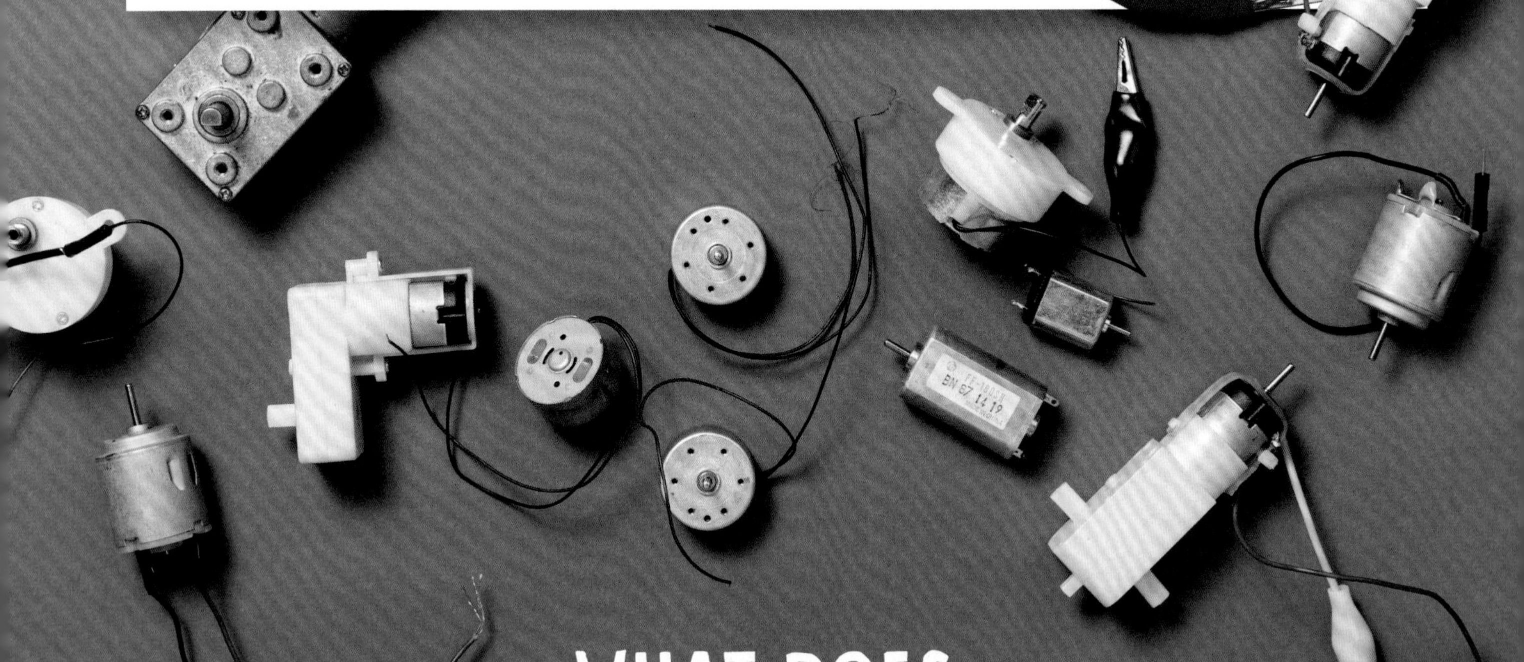

WHAT DOES RPM MEAN?

RPM stands for "revolutions per minute" and is a way of saying how fast a motor turns by counting the number of times it spins in one minute. This number will change depending on the power and the load, so it's more of a guideline than an exact figure.

The yellow gear motors shown here are 140 RPM. Fast-moving hobby motors can be around 6000 RPM and can be used for brush bots. You might use motors as slow as 4 to 5 RPM. Each project will have different needs, so choose the best motor for the job.

What can you do with a MOTOR right now?

Dissect a Motor

Try to open up an old motor and see what's inside. Can you take it apart? Can you make something out of the parts?

Power on the Motor

Connect the motor's wires to a battery pack by touching the metal ends of the wires to the top and bottom of a battery. You can use a rubber band to keep the wires in place. Listen for the faint humming of the spinning shaft inside the motor—sometimes it can be hard to hear.

Brush Bot

Take a fast-spinning motor and add a small piece of a hot glue stick to the end of the spinning shaft so that it makes an offset weight. Firmly attach the motor to a cleaning brush, sponge, or toothbrush and power on the motor with a battery. Notice how the unbalanced weight makes the bot vibrate, shake, and dance around the table.

Chain Reaction

Use a motor to create the starting point of a chain reaction machine. For example, a motor can move a skewer stick to knock down the first domino of a set that ends with a ball rolling down a track and landing in a bucket, which then . . . you get the idea!

Wire a Generator

Motors use electricity, but they can also work in reverse and generate electricity. Connect a motor to an LED. If the light doesn't glow, try a different LED or motor.

art robots

Use a motor and a battery to build a robot that draws! The possibilities are endless, and you can connect the parts in different ways to make surprising designs.

FIND THIS STUFF

Safety goggles | Round-nose pliers | Roll of 18-gauge stainless steel wire | Hobby gear motor with wires attached | Masking tape | Size 81 rubber band | AA battery | Metal container, recycled cup, small bowl, or other base | Table covered in white paper | Markers

GET STARTED

1. Wearing safety goggles, use pliers to cut a piece of wire and slip it through the hole in the motor shaft. Make a sharp bend in one end to keep it from coming back out.

2. Tape the bent end of the wire securely to the motor. Leave the long piece of wire loose on the other side. Twist it into a spiral.

3. Stretch the rubber band over the battery, from end to end.

4. Tape the motor and the battery to your base. Test the motor: Slip the end of each wire from the motor under the rubber band to touch the metal ends of the battery. The motor should run, turning the long twisted wire. Then, disconnect the wires.

5. Now it's time to see if you can make your robot move and draw patterns. Bend the twisted wire coming out of the motor so it hits the table. Attach a marker to the machine with another wire.

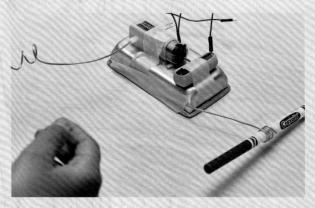

Experiment with pointing your wire in different angles so that you can make different designs.

PLAY & EXPLORE

Plug in the motor to the battery wires and see if your art robot will move. Bring your machine to the white paper, take off the marker cap, and see what designs it makes.

You can try many different ways to hold your marker. A wire works, but you could also try using a clothespin or even taping your marker directly to the base of your robot.

When your machine isn't drawing, be sure to put the cap back on the marker.

Look for interesting bases, like this tiny metal pot. See how the materials you choose can affect your design.

Make multiple art machines and let them dance and draw together. Pretty soon you'll see a beautiful artwork created by your robot art makers.

Figure out a way to prevent the machines from falling off the table with a cardboard border. Or you can design your robots so that they stop when they reach the edge of the table.

GO DEEPER ↓

GOING DEEPER

robotic masterpieces

Take your bots to art school and experiment with all the designs you can create with motors and batteries.

Painting Robot

Experiment with art supplies. You can make a robot that draws using a brush and washable paint, Q-tips and ink, crayons, or pencils. You might have to adjust the way your machine moves to take advantage of the type of drawing implement.

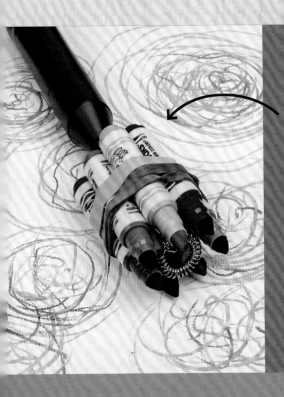

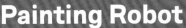

Experiment with Motors

For another recycled art machine, look for an old electric toothbrush or coffee frother. Attach markers so that they stand up and watch how the vibration of the motor makes the machine move and create new types of patterns.

S·T·E·A·M Connections
STICK & SLIP

Your robot can hop around the white paper and draw partly because of the slip-stick phenomenon. This happens when two materials come in contact with each other. It produces an irregular motion when they stick together and then another motion when they slide or slip apart. Observe your art robot to see if you can notice these two points. The different loops, squiggles, and vibrating lines your robot draws are partly due to the forces of slip-stick motion.

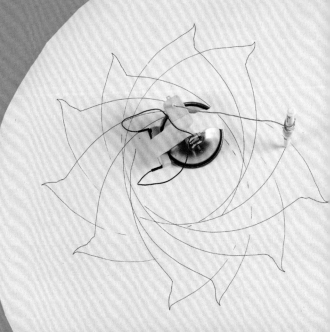

Groovy Patterns

Get a black light and place it above the table. Swap out the markers for highlighters or fluorescent paint for some glowing experiments.

Spin Art

Get inspired by this electronic project for kids from **Volt, Paper, Scissors!** Try building your own drawing machines with spinning paper platforms and rotating marker rigs.

ALUMINUM FOIL

Aluminum foil can do a lot more than wrap up candy, gum, and sandwiches. This thin metal sheet is not magnetic but is very conductive, which means that electricity can travel through it. Foil can be sculpted, ripped, cut with scissors, and shaped by hand. You can buy it in a roll or sheets at any grocery store. Tinkering projects are a great way to reuse foil!

WHY DO THE TWO SIDES OF FOIL LOOK DIFFERENT?

If you take a look at aluminum foil, you'll see that one side is dull and the other is more shiny. When the sheet of foil is made, a thicker piece gets separated in two. The sides facing each other on the inside are less bright and reflective than the ones on the outside.

What can you do with ALUMINUM FOIL right now?

Cookie Cutters

Use cookie cutters and aluminum foil to make cupcake pans in fun shapes. Wrap foil on the bottom and sides of cookie cutters. Fill with your favorite cake batter recipe, bake the cupcakes, and enjoy your delicious tinkering.

Ball It Up

Shape a piece of aluminum foil into a ball. Can you get it to roll? How can you smooth out irregular bumps and divots?

Foil Friend

Sculpt a piece of foil into the shape of a person. What do you notice when you build a figure out of foil?

METALLIC TAPE

Aluminum foil is the most common type of metallic sheet. There is also metallic tape, such as aluminum tape and copper tape, which can be used to make switches and electrical connections. Aluminum or copper tape can be found online and at shops that sell parts for electronics. Copper tape is also stocked at garden stores because it can keep snails away from growing herbs and veggies.

surprising switches

We use switches every day to turn on lights, play video games, or type emails. Try building your own switch out of aluminum foil.

FIND THIS STUFF

Battery-operated motor (add a toothpick flag to make it easier to see it spinning) | 3 wires with alligator clips | Aluminum foil | Battery pack with batteries

GET STARTED

1. Connect one of the wires from the motor to the foil (the yellow alligator clip shown below). Connect the other wire from the motor (the red alligator clip) to one of the battery wires.

2. Connect the other wire from the battery pack to the foil (the green alligator clip). The motor should start to spin and the flag will turn.

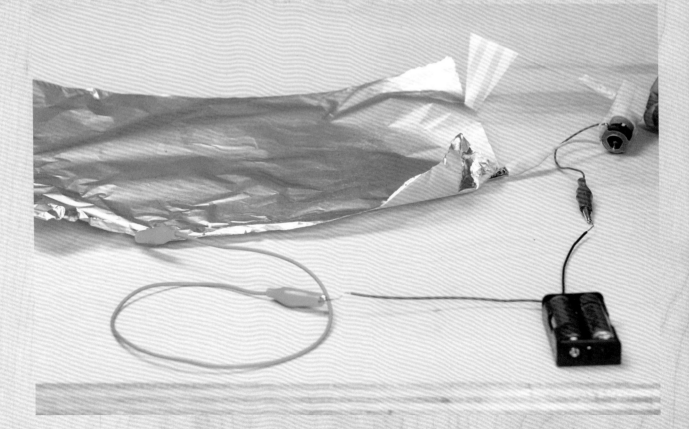

3. Break the circuit by cutting or ripping the foil apart so that the motor stops spinning.

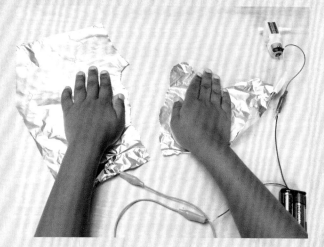

4. Press the metal together to restart the motor.

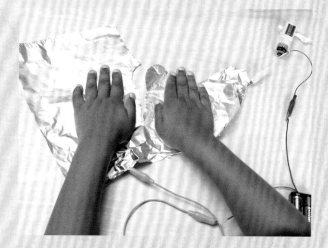

5. Fold a new piece of foil into a rectangular strip. Touch this between the two foil pieces to connect the circuit.

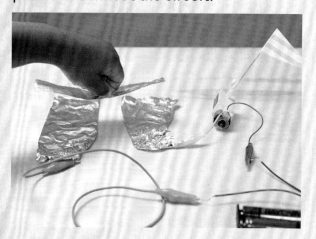

6. Switch the motor on and off by touching the foil strip to the foil pieces and then removing it. You made a foil switch!

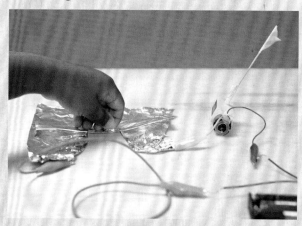

Sturdy Switch

Now that you know how to make Surprising Switches, try this sturdier version. Cut three rectangles out of cardboard for the switch pieces. Wrap foil over the cardboard to make it sturdier. Now try to turn it on and off.

Turn the page to find a fun project that uses this Sturdy Switch!

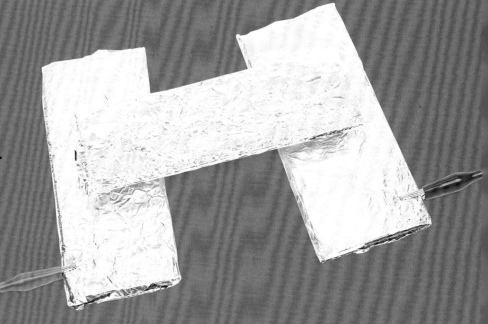

confetti drop

Mount a Sturdy Switch to the top of a door. Open the door to start a fun celebration!

FIND THIS STUFF

Painter's or gaffer's tape | Sturdy Switch (page 127) | Safety goggles | Round-nose pliers | Stainless steel wire | Wires with alligator clips | Battery-operated motor | Battery pack with two AA batteries | Clear container | Cardboard circle larger than opening of clear container | Colorful paper squares

GET STARTED

1. Tape the two side pieces of the Sturdy Switch to the wall over a doorframe. Attach the third connector piece to the top of the door with stainless steel wire and tape, as shown on the facing page. Adjust so the door swinging open touches the foil together and brings the connector in contact with the two side pieces, activating the switch.

2. Wearing safety goggles, use pliers to cut a piece of wire. Slip it through the motor shaft, fold over one side, and tape it to the spinning part. On the other end of the wire, attach the cardboard circle.

3. Fill the container with paper confetti. Tape the motor, with its cardboard circle, to the container. Set it up so that the cardboard blocks the opening but moves out of the way when the motor spins. It's okay if you spill some confetti. When it's ready, tape the setup to the top of the doorframe.

4. Connect the wires from the switch to the battery to the motor and back to the switch again, making a circuit. Use tape to keep it all in place. Open the door to see if the foil pieces touch and some confetti drops.

5. Invite someone to swing the door open, and wait for a surprise confetti drop!

PLAY & EXPLORE

See how you can arrange your motor, cardboard, and wires so that the switch triggers a confetti drop when the door opens.

Depending on which way the motor is connected to the battery, it will spin in a certain direction. If it's spinning the wrong way, just switch up the wires.

Sometimes the switch may not easily turn on with the door swing. And sometimes the switch may get stuck in the on position and won't go back to off when you want. The best way to fix this is to test early and often. Get different people to try your switch and observe to see how it works.

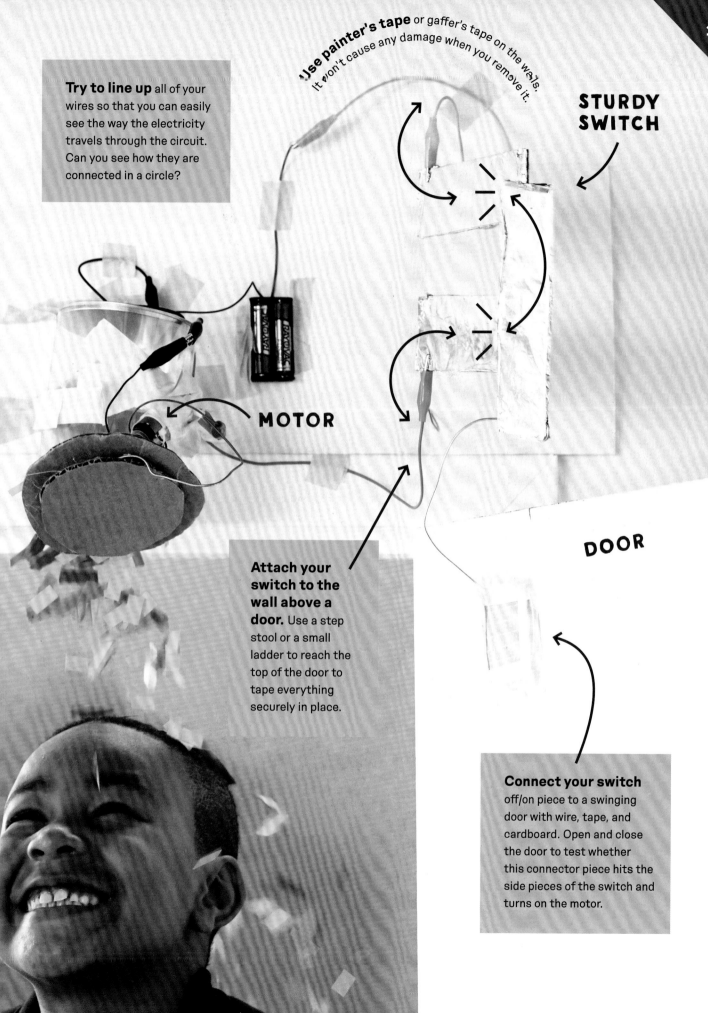

Try to line up all of your wires so that you can easily see the way the electricity travels through the circuit. Can you see how they are connected in a circle?

*Use painter's tape or gaffer's tape on the walls. It won't cause any damage when you remove it.

STURDY SWITCH

MOTOR

Attach your switch to the wall above a door. Use a step stool or a small ladder to reach the top of the door to tape everything securely in place.

DOOR

Connect your switch off/on piece to a swinging door with wire, tape, and cardboard. Open and close the door to test whether this connector piece hits the side pieces of the switch and turns on the motor.

LEDs

LEDs are little glowing lightbulbs that come in many colors, shapes, and sizes. They can be as tiny as a grain of rice or as big as a gumdrop. You can find them in remote controls, traffic lights, or high-tech fashion. LEDs can fade, blink, or even change color. They provide light and color to paper- and fabric-based tinkering projects, but they can light up entire buildings and make illuminated art that spans giant bridges. You can find LEDs online, or you can pull them from old electronics, Christmas tree lights, or fairy lights.

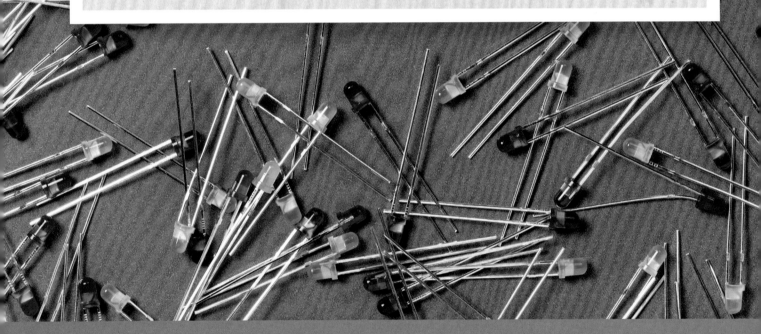

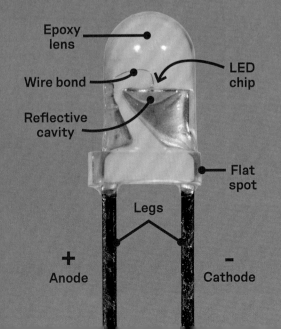

Epoxy lens

Wire bond

Reflective cavity

LED chip

Flat spot

Legs

+
Anode

-
Cathode

WHAT DO THE LETTERS L-E-D STAND FOR?

You don't have to know how an LED works to use one in your projects. But if you're curious, here's a simple explanation. The L stands for light. The light is sent out or emitted (the E) when electrons pass through a special material called a semiconductor. The D stands for diode. A diode is a type of tiny switch that allows electricity to flow in only one direction. So your LED will turn on only when it's connected to the battery in the right way.

What can you do with LEDs right now?

Power Up an LED

Grab a 3-volt coin cell battery and attach one leg of an LED to each side. If it doesn't work, flip the light around and try again. How many LEDs can you power in this way with one battery?

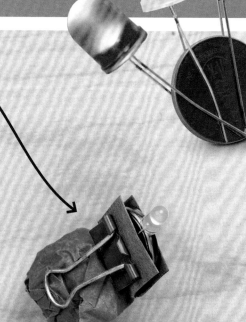

Throwie

Make an LED pack by sandwiching a coin cell battery with an LED light between two pieces of cardboard, securing them with a clip. Add a loop of tape or a magnet to the pack to make a "throwie," or sticky light, that you can toss into hard-to-reach places to add a glowing light.

Scavenge LEDs

Did you know you don't always have to buy new LEDs? Look for battery-powered light-up toys, solar garden lamps, and mini flashlights at garage sales or secondhand shops. Dissect them to find different types of LEDs that you can snip off and reuse in your tinkering projects.

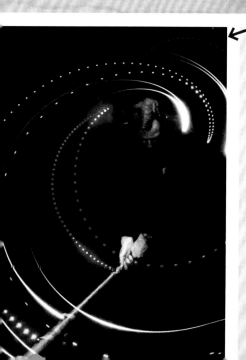

Light Painting

If you have a camera with a long exposure setting or a light painting app for your phone or tablet, you can take photos that trace the path of a moving light. Attach LEDs to a bicycle wheel, hula hoop, or baseball bat. Step into a dark room, move the object, and take a photo that captures the path of light. You can experiment with blinking LEDs for a fun effect, too.

Flower Diffusion

Find materials that have translucent properties. That means that when you put them next to a light, they glow. Some examples could be packing peanuts or plastic bags. Can you make a light-up flower using these materials and an LED?

glow city

Mixing circuits and cardboard to build a city is a great way to start exploring the world of crafting with LEDs. In this project, flat copper tape takes the place of wire. The electronics of paper circuits can be simple, starting with a single LED and battery.

FIND THIS STUFF

Scissors or utility knife | Cardboard | Roll of copper tape | CR2032 3-volt coin cell battery | Masking tape | Several LEDs (the big 10-mm ones are fun, but any will do) | Hot glue gun

GET STARTED

1. Using scissors or a utility knife, cut out four pieces of cardboard for the walls of a building. On one of the cardboard walls, create your circuit. Peel off the paper backing from the copper tape and stick two lines about 1 inch apart from each other (make sure they don't touch).

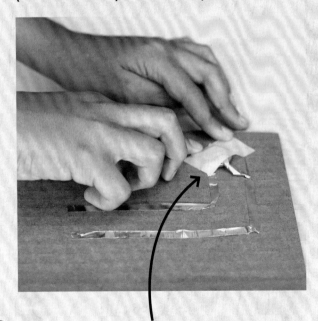

2. Place a coin cell battery on the end of one of the lines of tape. Peel back the end of the other line and place the nonsticky side on top of the battery. Add masking tape to keep everything in place.

3. Touch the two metal legs of an LED to the copper tape lines, with one leg on one line and the second leg on the other line. Does it light up? If not, you might need to switch which leg touches which line. When it's working, tape the LED on with extra copper tape.

4. Glue the walls together to make your building. Be sure the circuit is on the inside. Repeat the steps and build more structures to make a city.

Add a roof and other decorations to your glowing buildings.

PLAY & EXPLORE

Cut out windows and doors in your buildings. Cover them with parchment paper, tracing paper, or white felt to allow the light to shine though.

Test out special types of LEDs that blink, flash, and change color. Can you make it look like a party is happening in one of the houses?

Play with shadows of the LED lights on windows. You can add objects inside to create a mini shadow scene.

Add other elements to your city. What about a blinking traffic light or a taped-down road?

Keep going with your creations until you've built a giant city with all sorts of different structures and stories.

Add more LEDs to the copper tape lines in the same way as the first one. Not all colors of LEDs work together, so you'll have to test things out to get the combinations right.

GO DEEPER ↓

hand-crafted circuits

Explore ways you can combine LEDs with materials that are easy to use and find. There are so many ways to customize your Glow City.

Ins & Outs

Experiment with other inputs and outputs for your Glow City. You can use motors to make elements move, or try sending electricity to your creations with a solar light or a hand-crank generator.

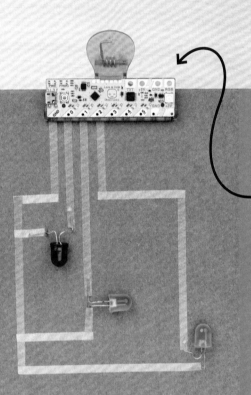

Programmable Elements

You can try out easy-to-use programming tools to make your Glow City lights blink, fade, or change colors. **Chibitronics** makes chips and clips that are good for beginners. The hardware connects to copper or fabric tape and the coding interface lends itself to tinkering. This company also makes circuit stickers you can integrate into your projects.

Tinkering Inspirations
CRAFTING WITH CIRCUITS

Artist and engineer **Jie Qi** combines traditional handicrafts with new technologies like LEDs, sensors, and controllers. Combining crafts like paper folding, ceramics, and woodworking with new technologies requires lots of tinkering. Jie has invented things like flat LED stickers that can fit into homemade greeting cards and a little computer in the shape of a binder clip to connect to pop-up paper projects. Jie says her process requires lots of "playing around and often not knowing if something is going to turn out a certain way."

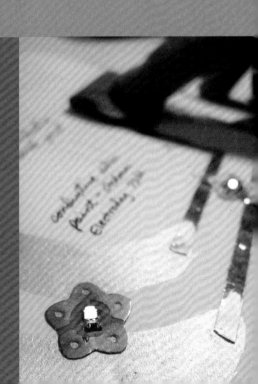

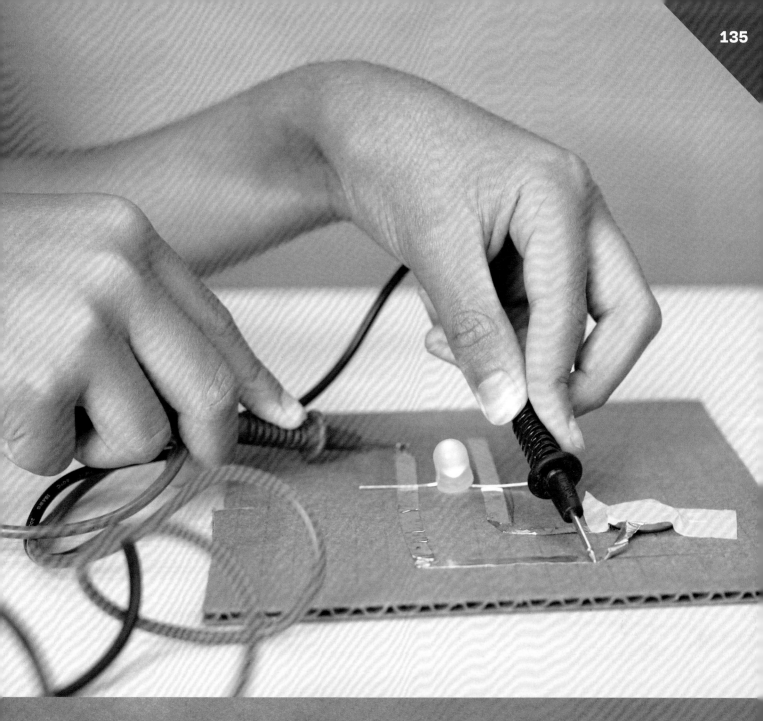

Multimeter

This handy tool can help you craft circuit projects. When using the **continuity detector** setting, which usually looks like a little speaker symbol, the multimeter beeps if the circuit is connected. This tests for a **short circuit**, which means the electricity can travel back to the battery without going through the LED.

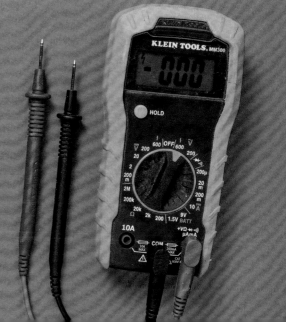

CHAPTER 7
wind & water

What happens when you inflate a plastic bag friend, rearrange recyclables so they spin in the wind, build a floating raft out of natural materials, or trigger a water-powered chain-reaction machine?

PLASTIC BAGS

Tons of plastic bags are used every day around the world, and they never fully decompose. For your tinkering projects, collect, reuse, and remake them into something new. You can reuse bags from the supermarket, take-out restaurants, or retail stores. Keep them in your workshop and sort by size, color, or transparency (see-through versus opaque).

WHAT DO THE NUMBERS MEAN?

There are two numbers to keep in mind when you want to know the size and thickness of the bag. The first is the capacity of the bag, which is measured in liters or gallons. The second is the thickness of the bag, which is measured in mils, which are 1/1000th of an inch. A kitchen trash bag is around 0.9 mil, and a heavy-duty trash bag is about 3 mils.

What can you do with PLACE PLASTIC BAGS right now?

Chain Art

Weave strips of plastic bags in and out on a chain-link fence, a bike wheel, or other metal frames.

Streamers

Cut bags into strips that can blow in the wind. Tie them to a dowel or to your bike handlebars.

Plastic Parachute

Attach a plastic bag to a clothespin or washer with string. Drop it from a high place and watch the parachute fall. Can you change the design so that the parachute spins or flips on the way down?

Make a Kite

Make a frame out of dowels or skewer sticks and add a layer of plastic on top for a homemade kite. Don't forget to tie on a long piece of string! Test out different designs and see what works best to fly the kite high in the sky.

Trash Tutu

Cut a plastic bag into strips, then attach the strips to a band of elastic to make a trash tutu. Can you overlap different colors, sizes, and textures?

inflatable friends

Have you seen inflatables waving in front of stores or car dealerships? With recycled plastic bags and some creativity, you can make your own version of these flyers that trap air and move in the wind. Discover how air moves, how plastic responds to pressure, and the strength of connections.

FIND THIS STUFF

Scissors | Colorful plastic bags | Masking tape | Plastic bottle | Hair dryer with a cool air setting

GET STARTED

1. Create the body of your inflatable friend by using scissors to cut two matching shapes out of plastic bags.

2. Arrange the cutouts one on top of the other. Seal the edges with tape, but leave a small opening on one bottom corner.

3. Cut the bottom off the plastic bottle so that the top of the bottle fits over the mouth of your hair dryer.

4. Tape the top of the bottle to the hole in the bag. This makes an air funnel for filling your inflatable with air.

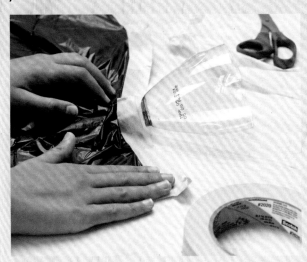

5. Insert the blow dryer into the open end of the bottle, turn it on (at a cool setting), and watch your friend inflate! Check to make sure that the air stays trapped in the plastic body.

Safety Note: Make sure your hair dryer is on the cool setting. If it blows hot air, you can melt the plastic. If you can't find a hair dryer with a cool setting, use a small fan to inflate your friend.

PLAY & EXPLORE

You can use fishing line or string to hold up your inflatable sculpture so that you can more easily test it.

Test your inflatable by turning your hair dryer on and off and watching it fill with air.

Make horns, tentacles, or arms. Cut two pieces of plastic of the same shape and tape them together. Cut a hole in the body and insert the new body parts, taping them well so no air can escape. Keep adding more parts and shapes until you're happy with your design.

Masking tape or googly eyes make a face come to life.

Customize your friend with fabric, ribbon, or frayed strips of paper.

Can you create long legs, curves, or or big ears?

Think about the shape of the inflatable. It can go straight up like a wind-sock character or a giant cac-tus or out to the side like a spider.

If your inflatable doesn't fill with air, run your hand over the edges and see where you feel air escaping. Patch any holes with extra tape.

GO DEEPER ↓

GOING DEEPER

air-filled fun

Discover new ways you can use fans, hair dryers, and the wind outside to play with inflatables, balloons, and fashion.

Outdoor Inflatable

Take your plastic bags outside and see if you can use wind or blowing air to activate your creature.

Inflatable Fashion

You can embed small battery-powered fans in your clothes. Think about how the inflatables may interact with fabric and what special effects you'd like to design.

Hot-Air Balloon

Have you ever watched a hot-air balloon rise up in the sky? If you go to a hot-air balloon festival, you can take a close look at how the balloons fill with air and rise with the heat from the flames.

Tinkering Inspiration
BIOMIMICRY FASHION

Want to add a bit of biology to your tinkering projects? You can get ideas from artist and scientist **Amisha Gadani**, who designed this inflatable dress, inspired by a blowfish, that doubles as a kinetic sculpture. Amisha rigged up tiny fans to inflatable pouches and triggered them with a switch hidden in her hand to mimic the animal's defenses. In this way, the dress shows a form of biomimicry, which is a term that describes how natural processes and designs can inspire human-made projects and inventions.

Giant Creatures

Get inspired by artist **Shih Chieh Huang** and build a big creature out of large plastic bags and attach the ends to a box fan. Watch how it moves and dances in the wind. What's different about working with stronger plastic and more powerful fans?

S·T·E·A·M Connections
DENSITY OF AIR

When inflatables float or sink, the key idea is the density of the air. This means how many molecules can fit into the space. When filled with a gas that's less dense than air, like helium, an inflatable rises up. Air becomes less dense when it's heated, which is why a hot-air balloon rises. Other setups like your inflatable friends are trickier. They are rigid when they are filled because the plastic structure gives them stability.

HOT AIR

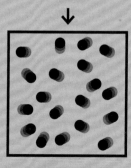

COLD AIR

RECYCLED CUPS

Recycled cups and other food and drink containers can be used for so many tinkering projects. Save and collect yogurt cups, paper coffee cups, and other paper and plastic containers for your art and science explorations. Find a cardboard box for storing your collection of containers. Be sure to rinse them with water before saving them for your tinkering projects.

Drawing Top

Stick a marker through the middle of a cup and spin it like a top. Can you make changes that affect the pattern the cup draws on paper?

Telephone

Connect two cups with a piece of string to make a low-tech walkie-talkie. Can you hear someone whispering through the string?

What can you do with RECYCLED CUPS right now?

Store Supplies

Store small tinkering materials like LEDs, hardware, or googly eyes in recycled cups of all sizes. Label the containers so you can remember what goes where.

Cup Character

Build a character using colorful paper, googly eyes, or any other craft materials you have around the house. You can cut or combine recycled cups to make octopuses, snakes, or penguins.

Seed Starting

Start seeds by filling a cup with soil, poking in a seed, and watering it every now and then. Set your seed cups in different places to observe the effects of different temperatures and light exposure. If the seeds sprout and the seedlings get big enough, you can transplant them outside.

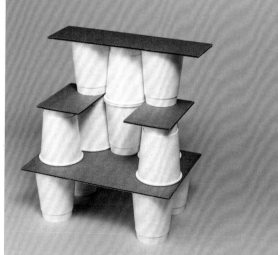

Stack Cups

Grab some cups and start stacking. If you add cardboard layers in between the cups, you might be able to make a structure that can support your weight. Can you build something strong enough that you can sit or stand on it?

wild Windmills

Explore how paper and plastic cups can catch the wind and spin with DIY windmills. Colorful recycled cups twirl around in front of a fan or outside on a windy day. There are endless possibilities to make something that spins quickly, slowly, or smoothly.

FIND THIS STUFF

Hot glue gun | Scrap wood | Masking tape | Straw | Recycled paper or plastic cup | Scissors | Dowel or skewer stick that can spin freely inside the straw | Small piece of plastic (from a soda bottle or yogurt cup)

GET STARTED

1. Make a base for your windmill by hot-gluing one piece of scrap wood upright on another. Tape the straw to the top so that it hangs a bit over the sides.

2. To turn your cup into a windmill, cut diagonal strips in the edges and fold them back. There are many different designs you can try.

3. Poke a skewer stick or dowel into the windmill cup (or attach it with hot glue). Cut a circle of plastic, poke a hole in its middle, and slip it onto the skewer or dowel. The plastic disk will sit between the straw and the cup, allowing the cup to spin freely without catching on the straw. Slip the skewer or dowel through the straw. Give it a spin!

4. Test out your creation! Place it in front of a fan or outside on a windy day and see if it spins.

PLAY & EXPLORE

There are a lot of different forces at play with the windmill so it might not spin as expected. That's okay—you can improve it! Spin the windmill with your finger and try to see where it gets stuck.

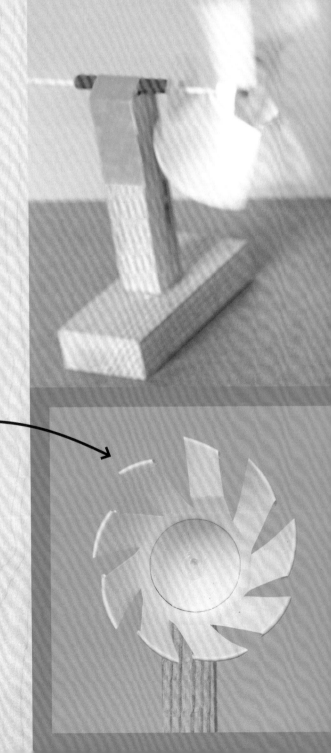

Try out different windmill designs. You can cut the cup into different shapes or use cardboard or skewer sticks to extend the blades.

Curved shapes and angled blades catch the wind, but you can also use more irregular shapes. What is the most unusual design you can make that actually spins?

How does the material affect the way the windmill spins? Try using recycled cups that are more or less flexible to see which ones work best.

See how big or small you can make your windmill. Is there a design that goes faster in the stream of air?

Change the angle and location of the fan. Does the windmill spin better when the air is blowing straight on, upward, downward, or from the side?

GO DEEPER ↓

keep on spinning

What new elements can you add to your spinning windmills? Think about how your designs are related to real-world turbines and waterwheels.

Paper Pinwheels

Fold a paper pinwheel (look for origami designs online). See how it spins in the wind. Try out different folded shapes and colored papers.

Windmill Whirligig

Many types of whirligigs create interesting motions with color and shape. Try adding a wire crank to the end of the skewer or dowel to make a wind-powered automata.

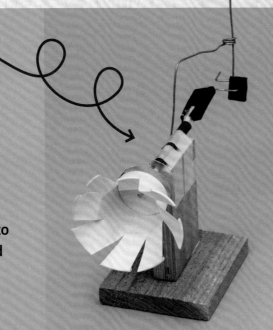

Waterwheel

Can you adapt your windmill design to be used as a waterwheel? Explore the ways in which you can use recycled cups to make a device that spins in a flowing stream or as part of your Water Factory activity on page 158.

S·T·E·A·M Connections
WIND ENERGY

Have you ever seen a wind turbine in a field near you? They convert the wind into electricity when the turbine turns. They are different from traditional windmills, which use the wind to help grind grain or pump water. Wind turbines make electrical energy. Windmills make mechanical energy.

As you make small changes in the design of your windmills, can you imagine how those little differences in your blades would have a big effect if they were made to large-scale wind turbines or windmills?

Outdoor Windmill

Can you build a windmill outside using other recycled materials for windmill blades? You could cut a plastic bottle and see if it spins. Or you could cut cardboard into blades and fasten them to a wooden post. Which materials can withstand gusts of wind and get wet without getting damaged?

CORK & FOAM

Cork is a natural material that is impermeable and buoyant. In other words, it floats on water but doesn't get wet on the inside. You can find used wine corks at reuse and swap shops and cork squares at craft stores. Rubber foam is a human-made, air-filled material that also floats on water. One easy-to-find form of foam is pool noodles, which can be sliced into disks and other shapes for tinkering projects.

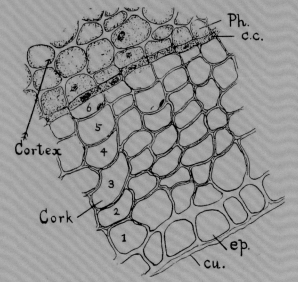

HOW DOES CORK FLOAT?

Cork is an amazing natural material that comes from a type of oak tree that grows mostly in Spain and Portugal. If you zoom way in on the structure of the cork, you'll see that the cells have a pentagonal or hexagonal honeycomb structure. These little pockets are full of an airlike mixture that gives the material its buoyant and elastic properties.

What can you do with CORK & FOAM right now?

Cork Chair

As tinkerer **Aaron Kramer** says, "Trash is a failure of imagination." Aaron found a lot of wine corks that were going to be thrown away and used them to make a comfy chair. What types of big structures could you build with a lot of corks?

Cork Characters

Balance a cork using two skewer sticks with weighted washer "feet" on the end. What kind of characters can you imagine? What can you add to make them more stable?

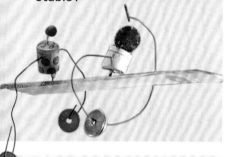

Foam Chandelier

Build a sculpture out of translucent and opaque packing foam. Place white LED or string lights inside the design. Can you make a recycled foam chandelier?

Art Stamps

Make a stamp by cutting out foam shapes and gluing them to a flat, sturdy material. Dip the stamp in ink or paint and then press onto paper.

float a boat

Build floating boats and watch how different materials move in the water. Your boats can be propelled by rubber bands, motors, sails, or fans. Make a design that can glide along the surface of the water without sinking.

FIND THIS STUFF

Large container (such as a basin, tub, kiddie pool, or plastic bin) | Water | Cork or foam | Rubber bands, toothpicks, straws, and recycled materials

GET STARTED

1. Fill a large container with water.

2. Build a stable base for your boat with cork or foam. You can tie corks together with rubber bands, connect cork squares with toothpicks, or wrap a circle of corks around a recycled water bottle. You can build endless variations of boats and rafts.

3. Place your boat in the water and see if it floats. Make adjustments as needed until your boat drifts across the water.

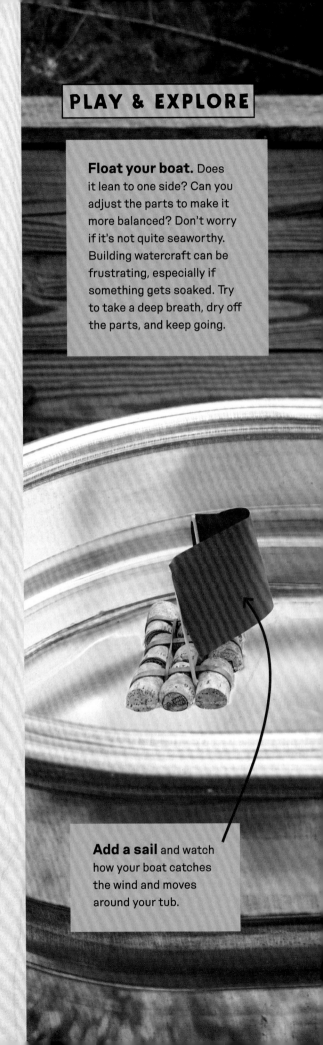

PLAY & EXPLORE

Float your boat. Does it lean to one side? Can you adjust the parts to make it more balanced? Don't worry if it's not quite seaworthy. Building watercraft can be frustrating, especially if something gets soaked. Try to take a deep breath, dry off the parts, and keep going.

Add a sail and watch how your boat catches the wind and moves around your tub.

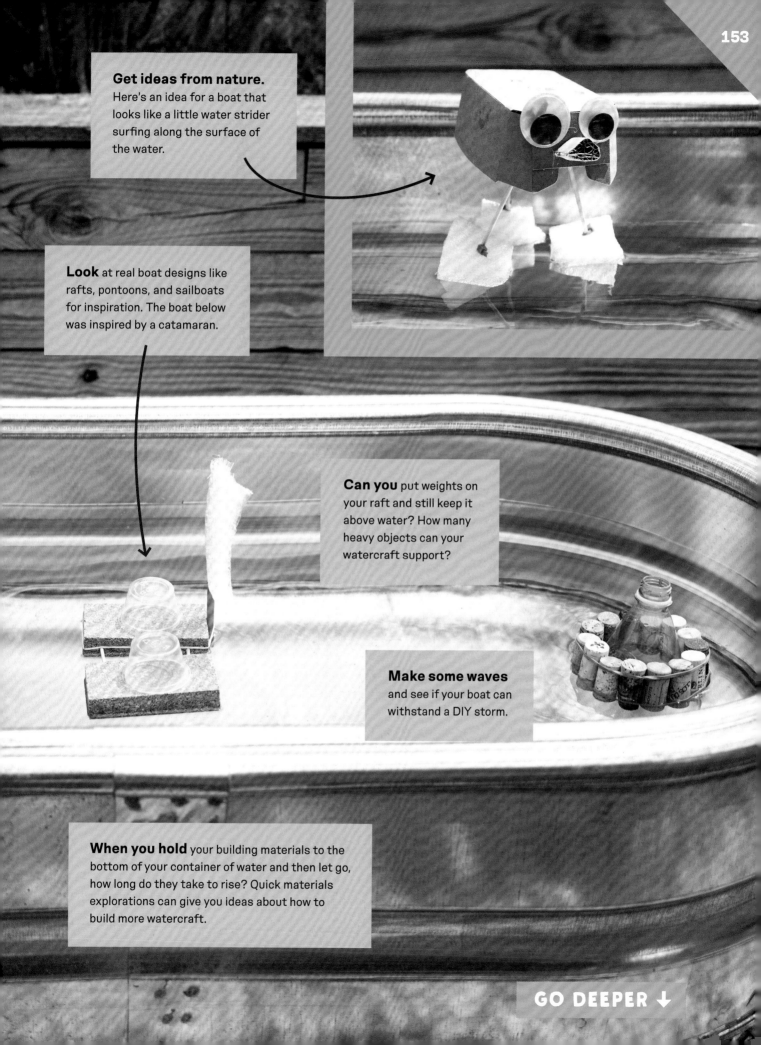

Get ideas from nature. Here's an idea for a boat that looks like a little water strider surfing along the surface of the water.

Look at real boat designs like rafts, pontoons, and sailboats for inspiration. The boat below was inspired by a catamaran.

Can you put weights on your raft and still keep it above water? How many heavy objects can your watercraft support?

Make some waves and see if your boat can withstand a DIY storm.

When you hold your building materials to the bottom of your container of water and then let go, how long do they take to rise? Quick materials explorations can give you ideas about how to build more watercraft.

GO DEEPER ↓

GOING DEEPER

remix your raft

Experiment with new materials to build boats that move around the water in interesting ways. There are many new directions to sail toward.

Beach Boats

Take a walk on the beach and collect materials that have washed ashore and might float. Test them out in the water. This way, you are cleaning the environment and making use of parts of buoys, surfboards, and wetsuits that were designed to float.

Art Boats

Here's an example of a boat that can blow bubbles with two programmable motors. Could your watercraft leave a trail of food coloring behind, transport small toys as part of a floating parade, or reflect the light of the water on the ceiling?

Rubber Band Boats

To make your boat move, you can try to make a paddle that's powered by a rubber band. Try something like this example with a plastic bottle, small cups, and rubber bands held in tension by skewer sticks.

S·T·E·A·M Connections
BUOYANCY BASICS

To make boats that float, we use a principle called buoyancy. The idea is that there is a force pushing on an object in water that's the same as the weight of the water that it displaced. Foam and cork have holes making them less dense than water, so they float. If something sinks, this principle means you can add light or hollow materials to it to make it float. When you add heavy objects like batteries and motors to your floater, you'll need to add enough low-density material to make your watercraft more buoyant.

Motor Boats

Add a battery and motor to make your boat go faster with an electric paddle. Make sure that you create a waterproof enclosure for the battery and motor. Try a plastic container with a tiny hole for the wires. After running the wires through the hole, seal it with hot glue.

PLASTIC TUBES

Tubes are hollow cylinders often made from metal, plastic, or cardboard. Typically, tubes are used to bring liquid or gas from one place to another. They can be big enough to walk inside or small enough to let only a water drop go through. There's a wide variety that you can find online or at hardware stores to experiment with, from PVC pipes to bendy tubes.

HOW TO CUT PVC

Here's a tool that lets you cut pipes and tubes safely. You clamp the tube inside the mouth at the place you want to cut so it's tight but still can spin. Then rotate the tool a couple of times, spin the knob to tighten, and rotate again. Repeat until you've cut through the tube.

What can you do with
TUBES
right now?

Sound Pipes

Flexible tubing makes an amazing sound when swirled in great circles around your head. Find a wide-open space and give it a try!

Stomp Rocket

A stomp rocket is made from a piece of PVC pipe, a piece of flexible tube, and a big plastic bottle. Stick the three pieces together, build a paper rocket, and stomp the plastic bottle to launch your creation into the sky.

Straw Viewer

Stretch a rubber band around a bundle of thick straws. Look through the viewer and notice how it changes your vision. Can you experiment with different sizes and lengths of tubes?

Pipe Sculptures

Use PVC pipe and a collection of angled connectors to construct sculptures. Can you build a fort you can go inside? This same technique will be used to make a frame for our water explorations on page 158.

water factory

Tubes and pipes can move flowing water around in whimsical ways. Test out different materials to bring water from point A to point B.

FIND THIS STUFF

10-foot length of ¾-inch PVC pipe | 4 T-shaped PVC connectors | 2 90-degree PVC elbows | Thick mesh material | Zip ties, clothespins, or rubber bands | Bucket or plastic bin of water | Plastic tubes, recycled bottles, funnels, rain gutters, and other water-carrying elements | Scrap pieces of plastic or foam | Pitcher or watering can for transporting water

GET STARTED

1. Construct a rectangular frame with PVC pipes, using T-shaped connector pieces and elbows to secure it, as shown on the facing page. Attach the mesh to the sides and top of the frame with zip ties so that it's sturdy enough to support your construction.

2. Place a bucket or bin of water at the base of your water factory so you're ready to test your ideas. Prepare to get wet!

3. Attach pieces of pipe, funnels, bottles, and whatever other elements you've chosen to your mesh wall with zip ties, clothespins, or rubber bands, to create a pathway for the water to travel from the top back down into the bucket or bin.

Safety Note: When you use zip ties, keep your fingers away from the part that tightens. Never close them around your fingers.

PLAY & EXPLORE

As you build, test out the water slide by pouring in some water and seeing if it flows down into the bucket or bin. You might need to make adjustments. Working with a constantly flowing material like water isn't easy.

Zip ties work well to attach elements to the water factory. Thread one side through the mesh, wrap it around the object, and then slip the end of the tie through the square locking mechanism and pull it tight. You can also try binder clips or rubber bands.

Add plastic or foam spacers in between the mesh layer and the tubes to help keep everything aligned.

Test out different entry points and pathways the water can take from the top to the bottom of the structure.

You can add supports to help make your elements more sturdy.

Now that the water is flowing, you can make elements that are activated by the flow of water. Some examples are waterwheels, levers, and spinners.

Can you invent a way to measure how much of the water makes it all the way down to the bucket at the end?

Collect interesting recycled containers of different colors and add them to your water factory.

GO DEEPER ↓

160

Water Works

Make a water pathway that has a playful purpose, like creating a unique way to quench your cat's thirst or water your plants.

Ping-Pong Run

Try sending a Ping-Pong ball from the top to the bottom of your water run. Can you speed up and slow down the ball? Can you adjust the way it rolls down? Are there places where it tends to get stuck? Try different elements and see how they can travel.

GOING DEEPER

water ways

There are many ways to customize your water factory. Change out your parts, add in new technology, and make the water do some work.

Slow the Flow

Design a vortex for water to get stuck swirling about inside. This could be made of a plastic bottle, tubes, or an old Frisbee. A spinning vortex creates a tornado shape in the water and can potentially slow down its path.

Water Pump

You can get a submersible pump that is powered by batteries or a USB cable. Place your pump inside the large container at the end of your track. Run a length of hose from the water out to the top of a wall and clamp it in place. Turn on the pump and design a circular system of water going from the bin to the hose and splashing back down into the bin.

S·T·E·A·M Connections
ANTIGRAVITY FLOW

Water normally flows down due to gravity, but we can change that if we use forces to act on the flow. A pump is one example of a device that can send water up to the top of the track. And, in fact, your body moving water with a watering can or pitcher also is expending energy to bring the water up.

As you build your water factory, can you make the water travel up an incline? You may be able to use the force of water pressure to make the water flow in unusual ways.

Water Power

Make your water system do some work for you. One example is to slowly fill up a container rigged to a pulley system to lift an object off the ground.

special thanks

Thanks to Nicole Catrett, Modesto Tamez, Erik Thorstensson, Jie Qi, Gever Tulley and Liam Nilsen for your advice and input on this book. Thanks to Claus Schneidereit for sharing your workshop and prototyping skills.

Thanks to my colleagues at the Tinkering Studio: Mike Petrich, Karen Wilkinson, Walter Kitundu, Luigi Anzivino, Nicole Catrett, Sebastian Martin, Ryoko Matsumoto, Mario Martinez-Muñoz, Lianna Kali, Kate Stirr, Deanna Gelosi, Jake Montano, Steph Muscat, and Michael Wong. Thanks to Anne Richardson for hiring me at the Exploratorium in the first place.

Thanks to Victoria von Ehrenkrook for tracking down Explo photo permissions. Thanks to Libby Catzcalo for help with Tinkering School photos. Thanks to Dale Dougherty, Sherry Huss and the Maker Faire team for welcoming me into the community of artists and tinkerers who have inspired so many projects in this book.

Thanks to Deanna Cook, Ian O'Neill, Hesh Hipp, Eliza Smith, Mars Vilaubi, Maddy Jackson, and the rest of the team at Storey Publishing for believing in this book and working hard to make it happen.

Thanks to my family and friends who cheered me on while writing. Thanks to Erica and Elio—I couldn't have created this project without your love and support. I'm excited to keep exploring and tinkering through life with you. And finally, thanks to my mom, who encouraged me as a child to see boredom as an opportunity, introduced the possibilities of playing with materials, and has inspired me every day since with her strength, determination, and independence.

Ideas about learning through tinkering inspired by:
Seymour Papert, Jean Piaget, Donald Schön, Jeanne Bamberger, Mitchel Resnick, Natalie Rusk, Eric Rosenbaum, Eleanor Duckworth, Cynthia Solomon, Edith Ackermann, Bruno Munari, Gever Tulley, Curt Gabrielson, Rachelle Doorley, Paul Tatter, Shirin Vossoughi, Meg Escudé, Bronwyn Bevan, Mike Petrich, Karen Wilkinson, Frank Oppenheimer, and many more.

Projects inspired by:
Nicole Catrett (18–19, 71, 99), Lianna Kali (18–19), Annabelle Nielsen and Kenn Munk of A Secret Club (18–19), Casey Federico (36), Steph Muscat (36), Corinne Takara (36), Sam Haynor (42, 88), Bea Rey (43), Walter Kitundu (43, 105), Hanoch Piven (45), Sam Wilde (49, 79), Sam van Doorn (51), Chabot Space & Science Center (51), Thomas Rees (51), Caine Monroy (54), Liam Nilsen (55), Gever Tulley, Julie Spiegler, and Robyn Orr of Tinkering School (64), Charlyn Gonda (65), Tim Hunkin (65), Alexander Calder (67), Marco Mahler and Henry Segerman (68), Samar Kirresh (70), Sterling Johnson (71), Amos Blanton (73), Montreal Science Centre (73), Sarah Wyman (78), Scout Tran (79), Cardboard Institute of Technology (79), Yuji Hayashi (79), Ryoko Matsumoto (80–83, 103) Sarah Alexander, Gary Alexander, Max Alexander, Lisa Finch, Celeste Moreno, Loulou Cousins, Mariana Tamashiro, Keith Braafladt, Jake Fee, and Mario Martinez-Muñoz (80), Federico Tobon (80), Paul Spooner, Lisa Slater, Carlos Zapata, Martin Smith, and Keith Newstead of Cabaret Mechanical Theatre (80), Concha Fernandez (83), New York Hall of Science (85), Emma Bearman (85), Pete Stephens (88), George Hart (90), Jonathan Bijur, Hanabee Cartagena, and Amara Leipzig of reDiscover Center (90), Noga Elhassid (92–95, 148), Shivani Singhal (94), Lenore Edman and Windell Oskay of Evil Mad Scientist Labs (98), Jode Roberts (99), Amanda Ghassaei (101), Denise King (104), Bob Miller (105), Amy Franceschini, Michael Swaine, and Stijn Schiffeleers of Future Farmers (105), Chris Bell (105), Gary Newlin (106–107), Karen Wilkinson (114), Carlotta Ferrozzi of ReMida Bologna (115), Sasha Pas (118), OliOli (122), Michael Scheuerl of Volt, Paper, Scissors! (123), Carmel Preschool (125), Colleen Graves (126), Amy Snyder, Sebastian Martin, and Paul Doherty (131), Leah Buechley, Jie Qi, Hannah Perner-Wilson, David Mellis, Emily Lovell, and Jennifer Jacobs of the High-Low Tech group at MIT Media Lab (132–135), Natalie Freed (134), The Tech Interactive (140–141), Amisha Gadani (142), Shih Chieh Huang (143), Tara Pratap Ebsworth and Jessica Strick (147), Vollis Simpson (148), Niklas Roy (149), Sebastian Martin (149), Celeste Moreno (151), Aaron Kramer (151), Erik Thorstensson, Lindsay Balfour, Olle Bjerkås, and Carl Bärstad of Strawbees (157), Paul Doherty (157), and Gregory Gavin of Riveropolis (158–159).

index

refraction, light, 103
robots. *See* Art Robots
roller toy, linkages and, 95
rope. *See* string and rope
rotary blade, 20
RPM, 118

S

sawhorse workbench, 19
sawing wood, 26
scale drawings, 94
scissors, 20
screwdriver, drill as, 27
screws, 44–49
   Forts, Flexible, 46–49
sculpture, 60–63, 85, 157
seating, 17, 18
sewing stuff, 18
shadow. *See* light and shadow
sign holder, 33
slip-stick phenomenon, 122
soldering, 29
sound machine, 83
stainless steel wire, 64–69
   activities with, 65
   gauge of, 64
   Wire Mobiles, 66–69
STEAM connections, 12
   action-reaction, 88
   angles, 48
   antigravity flow, 161
   balance, 62
   buoyancy, 154
   center of gravity, 42
   density of air, 143
   friction, 74
   light, science or, 114
   mirror math, 108
   probability, 55
   scale drawings, 94
   shadows, shifting, 102
   slip-stick phenomenon, 122

   stress and strain, 36
   torque, 68
   wind energy, 148
storage stuff, 18, 19
storytelling, 83
stress and strain, 36
string and rope, 70–75
   sculpture, dowel rope, 85
   Sky Trams, 72–75
Suncatchers, Bubble Wrap, 112–13
sun prints, 115
supplies, 14, 15. *See also specific type*
Switches, Surprising, 126–29
   building, 126–27
   Confetti Drop, 128–29

T

table setup, 16
tape, 22, 125
"throwie" sticky light, 131
tinkering station, 16–17
tool(s)
   awl, 21, 91
   cutting and snipping, 20–21, 156
   googly eyes and, 99
   handsaws, 26
   level, 41
   magnets, 45
   multimeter, 134
   pliers, round-nose, 24
   power drill, 26, 27
   practicing with, 39
   wire strippers, 25
tool organizer, 17
tops, 51, 91, 144
torque, 68
toy(s). *See also* characters; tops; Trams, Sky
   puppet, hand, 99
   roller, 95
toy hack, 36